FOCUS NO. 17   1985

ON EMPLOYMENT EQUITY

A CRITIQUE
OF THE

ABELLA
ROYAL COMMISSION
REPORT

By
Walter Block
and
Michael A. Walker

Ministry of Education, Ontario
Information Centre, 13th Floor,
Mowat Block, Queen's Park,
Toronto, Ont.   M7A 1L2

Ministry of Education, Ontario
Information Centre, 13th Floor,
Mowat Block, Queen's Park,
Toronto, Ont.   M7A 1L2

Canadian Cataloguing in Publication Data

Block, Walter, 1941 -
   On employment equity

   (Focus, ISSN 0715-5417 ; no. 17)
   ISBN 0-88975-088-2

   1. Canada. Royal Commission on Equality
in Employment. 2. Discrimination in
employment - Canada. I. Walker, Michael,
1945-   II. Fraser Institute (Vancouver,
B.C.) III. Title. IV. Series: Focus
(Fraser Institute (Vancouver, B.C.)) ; no. 17.
HD4903.5.C2C362 1985   331.13'3'0971
           C85-091499-X

COPYRIGHT ©1985 by The Fraser Institute. All rights reserved. No part of this book may be reproduced in any manner whatsoever without written permission except in the case of brief quotations embodied in critical articles and reviews.

Printed in Canada.

CONTENTS

ABOUT THE AUTHORS/v

CHAPTER 1: Introduction/1

CHAPTER 2: The Methodology of Discrimination/13

CHAPTER 3: The Economics of Discrimination/27

CHAPTER 4: A Statistical Analysis of Discrimination/41

CHAPTER 5: Jobs and Unemployment/63

CHAPTER 6: Equal Pay Legislation/69

CHAPTER 7: Job Training/79

CHAPTER 8: Conclusion/85

NOTES/91

ABOUT THE AUTHORS

WALTER BLOCK

Dr. Walter Block is Senior Economist at the Fraser Institute in Vancouver, British Columbia, and Director of its Centre for the Study of Economics and Religion. A member of the British Columbia Association of Professional Economists, the Canadian Economic Association, the Canadian Association for Business Economists, and an ex-university professor of economics, he has worked in various research capacities for the National Bureau of Economic Research, the Tax Foundation, and **Business Week** Magazine.

Dr. Block has published numerous popular and scholarly articles on economics. He is a regular contributor to **The Financial Post, Grainews,** and writes a syndicated column for Sterling newspapers. An economic commentator on national television and radio, he lectures widely on public policy issues to university students, service, professional, and religious organizations. Walter Block is the editor of the Fraser Institute books: **Zoning: Its Costs and Relevance** (1980); **Rent Control: Myths and Realities** (1981); **Discrimination, Affirmative Action, and Equal Opportunity** (1982); **Taxation: An International Perspective** (1984); **Theology, Third World Development, and Economic Justice** (1985); and is author of **A Response to the Framework Document for Amending the Combines Investigation Act** (1982); and **Focus: On Economics and the Canadian Bishops** (1983).

MICHAEL A. WALKER

Dr. Michael Walker, a native of Newfoundland, obtained his B.A. (summa) (1966) from St. Francis Xavier University, his M.A. (1967) and Ph.D. (1969) from the University of Western Ontario where he specialized in Mathematical Economics, Econometrics, and the theory of money. From 1969 to 1974 he worked in Ottawa at the Bank of Canada and as a Consultant to the policy branches of the Federal Department of Finance. He has taught Statistics and Monetary Economics at the University of Western Ontario and Carleton University.

Dr. Walker is a regular columnist in **The Financial Post,** the Sterling newspaper chain, and community newspapers across Canada. He prepares a daily, syndicated radio program called "Perspective" and these commentaries are published monthly in **Fraser Forum.** He speaks on a regular basis to a wide variety of groups, conferences, and associations throughout Canada and the U.S.

He is an author, editor, and contributor to articles and books on economic matters, e.g. **Balancing the Budget; Flat-Rate Tax Proposals; Reaction: The National Energy Program; Rent Control: A Popular Paradox; Unions and the Public Interest; Discrimination, Affirmative Action, and Equal Opportunity; Privatization: Theory and Practise;** and **Tax Facts.**

Dr. Walker is a member of the Mont Pèlerin Society, the Canadian and American Economic Associations, and the International Association of Energy Economists.

CHAPTER 1

INTRODUCTION

THE PLIGHT OF THE MINORITY

Nothing abuses a person's sense of natural justice more than unequal treatment of equals. In recent times, the existence of discrimination has increasingly troubled citizens and lawmakers. This concern has been expressed in the drive for "equal pay for equal work" (EPFEW) and "equal pay for work of equal value" (EPFWOEV) legislation, in the demand for affirmative action programs, and by the feminist movement itself.

Legislators have responded by establishing civil rights tribunals, issuing equal pay for equal work directives, and by engaging in a widespread program of affirmative action. In some cases, the latter has involved the establishment of quotas to ensure that people of different sexes, races, and ethnic backgrounds are proportionately represented in employment and educational situations.

Evidence on discrimination

The issues associated with discrimination and the legislative attempts to deal with it are highly emotional and, as a consequence, it is often difficult to discuss the subject dispassionately. However, there is mounting evidence, discussed below, that the attempts to eradicate what was thought to be discrimination are producing unforeseen and negative consequences. In some instances, the problems were inherently difficult to anticipate. In the vast majority of cases, however, they were perfectly predictable. The reason they were not foreseen is that analytical perspective was often lost in the haste to "right the wrongs" seemingly committed in the past.

This introduction offers an analytical perspective on discrimination and the programs proposed to end it in order to provide a backdrop against which to evaluate the Abella Report.

WHAT'S WRONG WITH DISCRIMINATION?

What is discrimination?

In the 1980s the term "discrimination" has acquired an unambiguously negative meaning. It conjures up the image of racial and/or sexual prejudice. Strictly speaking, however, the term is neutral in application. Discriminatory behaviour may have consequences which are benign, malevolent, or innocuous.

While it may appear pedantic to draw fine distinctions of this sort, it is of the utmost importance to do so. First of all, it must be recognized that discrimination is a natural part of everyday behaviour. We all like some foods and dislike others; most are attracted to beauty and repelled by ugliness; everyone finds interaction with some people more or less comfortable. The act of preferring one thing, one person, or one situation over another is an act of discrimination against all the non-preferred things, persons, or situations.

Discrimination defines individuality

Secondly, these acts of discrimination or preference are of more than superficial interest, since in a fundamental way, they define the limits of individuality. While we may speculate about "what makes some people tick," in the final analysis we assess people as individuals by the choices they make, or fail to make, and the actions which follow from those choices. Moreover, individuality and the right of human beings to make choices are a fundamental characteristic of free societies and, presumably, ought to be preserved to the greatest extent possible.

So, to answer the question posed at the outset, discrimination is nothing more than the expression of a preference. And in that neutral sense, without assessing the consequences of the behaviour, the right to discriminate is a desirable feature of free societies.

Majorities vs. minorities

Individual acts of choice may sometimes result in a majority preference which excludes or inconveniences some minority. For example, the majority of people are right-handed and, hence, most languages are written from left to right -- a convention which, while convenient for right-handers, means ink stained hands or cramped styles for south paws. Also school children are often observed to form a clique at the expense of some outcast children who differ in some physical or behavioural way from the rest of the group.

By the same token, the expression of preferences by a minority group may sometimes exclude the majority. Many segregated neighbourhoods, clubs and societies are instances where a group of people conspire to express their individuality by blantantly rejecting the majority. This is particularly true of religious societies and associations which also typically have a strict internal hierarchy so as to discriminate new from long-standing members. Examples include the Masons, the Knights of Columbus, Hell's Angels, the Shriners, Rotarians, Black Panthers.

Discriminatory enactments

Sometimes the majority may cause laws to be passed which institutionalize discrimination. Such enactments need not be limited to, or even purposefully aimed at, any particular racial, sexual, or ethnic categories. When the majority votes for a military draft, for example, minorities who are opposed -- specific racial, sexual, or ethnic characteristics notwithstanding -- are forced to go along. Pacifists are perhaps singled out in this case, but the law is neutral with regard to other characteristics.

Other examples of majority rules suppressing minority interests abound. Most central Canadians support tariff and trade barriers which protect inefficient industrial jobs in Ontario and Quebec; but people in the less well-populated Atlantic and Prairie provinces are forced to purchase high-cost manufactured goods, and suffer as a result. A majority of citizens in North America have voted for building codes; but these interfere with the rights of owners to do with their property as they please (even if they adhere to the proscriptions against nuisance).

Majority discrimination

The untoward aspects of discrimination that people are familiar with -- and which give discrimination such a bad name -- are usually of this majority rule variety.

There is no doubt that the majority can use the system of laws to exploit and disadvantage minorities. This is -- or at least certainly has been -- a problem. It was the law which restricted black minorities to separate and vastly inferior restroom facilities in the southern U.S. from the post Civil War period until midway into the twentieth century. Legislation prohibited minorities who wanted to engage in "intermarriage" -- and these laws continued until about the same period. European Jews too have had a long history of being legally restricted from entering certain professions and even industries.

Does this mean that minorities are doomed to their fate at the hands of the majority? It does indeed, if the majority is able to harness the power of the political process in its quest to subjugate the minority. Given this disadvantage, the minority is in a singularly unenviable position -- in jobs, in schools, in restaurants, and indeed, with regard to almost every aspect of existence that makes life worth living. For this reason, all societies which have some form of democratic rule must be constantly vigilant to ensure that the inherent power of the majority is not used legislatively to limit the freedom of minorities.

Minorities doomed?

But what about activities outside the sphere of legislation? A majority which is predisposed to discriminate will surely do so whether discriminatory treatment is codified in laws or not. Thus, whether inside the system of laws or outside it, minorities seem doomed to shabby treatment at the hands of the majority.

There is, however, a great difference between the forms of discrimination possible when the laws of the land conspire against minorities and when they do not. The difference is the coercive power of the state. If the law says blacks must ride in the back of the bus, or that minority group members may not intermarry, or that Jews must live in certain areas, the state has the power to ensure that these minorities comply. On the other hand, discriminatory behaviour not enshrined in law cannot be physically enforced since the use of compulsion by private citizens is not normally condoned. This is not to say the individuals have not used or do not continue to use force against minorities -- indeed there are daily instances of it. However, anti-racial or other anti-minority violence not condoned by law is regarded as criminal behaviour.

Criminal activity aside, how much discrimination can or will exist if there is no law against such behaviour and no law reinforcing it? Basically, this will depend on how strongly people feel -- that is, how strong are their preferences for discrimination.

THE ECONOMIC PERSPECTIVE

Discrimination -- a form of choice

Except in rare instances, people's preferences are not absolute. Rather, they are malleable over a fairly wide range. Under different circumstances, different choices would be made. One of the circumstances that has a substantial effect is the cost or benefit of making that choice. In general terms, the higher the cost (the lower the benefit), the less likely the choice will be made.

Individuals who prefer imported beer and would like to discriminate against the domestic variety may cease to do so when the price differential between the two products rises high enough. A rich aunt, whose maladroit social behaviour makes her unacceptable as a bridge partner, may be accepted by some nieces and nephews if the cost of excluding her were reciprocal exclusion from her will. Similarly, those inclined to discriminate among individuals according to race, sex, or colour may cease to do so if the cost is great. Conversely, if the cost is low or non-existent, then even people with only the slightest tendency to do so will be inclined to discriminate.

As we shall see below, sexual, racial, or ethnic discriminators must pay for their preference just like those who discriminate against domestic beer. Discrimination has a price. It will be demonstrated that the existence of this price tends to limit the amount of discrimination and to reduce the financial and other costs that minority groups would otherwise suffer.

In the market, discrimination costs money

How, and in what way, must discriminatory practice be paid for? Suppose employers were smitten with a sudden prejudice against redheads and either lowered their salaries or refused to hire them. The initial effect would be greater unemployment and lower wages for this newly created downtrodden group and, potentially, lower profits for the employers. Having rejected redheads as employees, the employers would have to hire more brunettes, blonds, and black-haired employees to take their places. In at least some instances -- perhaps many -- the replacements would be less effective in their jobs than the redheads, with the consequence that employer profits would be reduced.

Since there is no reason to believe that the productivity of people with red hair is different from that of other folk, forces would soon be brought to bear which would move the situation for redheads back toward the one that prevailed before the sudden onset of discrimination. For with a pool of under-employed and underpaid redheads, there would be great profits to be made by employing them! Colourblind employers (those who have no preference for or against people with any particular hair colour) would begin to hire redheads, and so would employers for whom the foregone profits represent too high a cost for them to indulge their preference for discrimination.[1]

These employers will not necessarily be motivated by benevolence. If all employees originally earned $400 per week and redhead wages were reduced to $300 by the onset of discrimination, the colourblind firm will not offer the redhead $400. Why should it? All it need do is offer $305 or any small increment above the lower salary to which the redhaired person has been reduced. The unfortunate redhead will have little choice but to accept, and the employer can garner huge benefits. (If it is worthwhile to hire the redhead at $400, it will be immensely profitable to employ an equally productive redheaded worker at $305.)

The ceaseless quest for profits

In their turn, other employers will also seek to hire the low-paid redheaded employees. True, they will have to offer more than the prevailing $305. Their sense of propriety may be offended by offering high wages to people they see as despicable redheads. They will, nevertheless, be comforted by the thought that it is better for them to earn extra revenues from employing additional redheads (even at the unconscionably high wages of $310, for example) than to leave them to the tender mercies of their current employer, even if the latter is earning a larger profit by employing them for $305. (It is better, in other words, for "me" to take $90 than for "you" to receive $95 in pure profit.)

Such thoughts will strike all other potential and actual employers. It will set up a process of raiding and counter-raiding, which will bid up redhead wages at each step. Where will it end? There is only one ultimate destination: the $400 earned by other equally productive employees.[2] Of course the wage and employment situation may not reach this theoretical configuration, but it will always tend toward it. Unwittingly, profit seekers will gradually reduce all gaps between the wages of redheads and others of equal productivity. (This is achieved, as we have seen, by "exploiting" these gaps; by hiring and offering higher wages to the undervalued redhead.) There is, therefore, a tendency for the self-interested action of profit seekers to ensure that persons who are subject to discrimination will not suffer financially from this affliction.

Prejudice not profitable

In the quest for profits, those employers who indulge their hair colour preferences will obviously pay for this choice. The price of their prejudice is the profit they must forego. Some employers may be willing to pay this price, and their discriminatory behaviour will thus not be eliminated -- until, that is, other non-discriminating, or less discriminating employers are able to drive them to the wall by underselling. However, the existence of other employers more sensitive to the cost of discriminating means that redheads will not have to suffer the degree of unemployment or low wages that would otherwise be the consequence even in the short run. The key to the redheads' escape from the full force of prejudice is their ability to offer other employers a profit possibility in the form of lower wages.

The dollar vote or the political vote?

Coercive discrimination imposed by law provides no such escape route. The majority doesn't have to bear the costs of its actions, as it would in the private sector. And this naturally short-circuits the normal financial incentive escape path for the minority.

From the point of view of a disadvantaged minority, the cherished majority rule feature of democracy becomes a tyranny, allowing the law to undermine it. The marketplace, on the other hand, at least provides the minority group member with the possibility that the situation will improve, or not worsen so radically in the first place.[3] In the case of discriminatory laws, the minority must first seek to become the majority, or at least to convince the majority to vote appropriately. In the case of economic undertakings, only one or a few persons need to be convinced, and their own selfish financial interest gives them incentive to in effect help the minority.

The back of the bus

Let us take the institution of "riding in the back of the bus" as a further illustration. This was a particularly vicious phenomenon, not so much because blacks rode in the rear (many people, after all, voluntarily choose this locale) but because they were forced to do so by law.[4] The stigma attached to this practice was psychologically debilitating and was particularly resented by black people.

If this had occurred not through force of law but simply because the bus company had decided to discriminate, a process of amelioration would have been set in motion. Other potential suppliers of bus services, seeing that blacks would willingly pay a higher price to be able to sit at the front of the bus, would have offered blacks their choice of seats! Such a competitor could have charged blacks higher fares than they paid for "rear only" service and still have been able to attract customers. But this option was closed off since state law prohibited then, and still prohibits now, the creation of alternative and competitive bus companies.[5] Blacks instead had to wait and suffer through many years of this practice before the social climate became such that it could be ended through the political process.

COMPETITION — THE GREAT EQUALIZER

Discrimination in employment

While, clearly, the search for profit will cause some employers to set aside their taste for discrimination, it is nevertheless true that others may be willing to incur the cost. However, the extent to which the most discriminatory employers can continue this behaviour will be largely determined by factors beyond their control, namely, by the competitive pressures exerted by other employers.

If, in general terms, the employer is protected from competition -- for instance, a public utility or a government agency -- the normal economic inhibitions against discrimination fail. In the case of public utilities, profits are regulated and costs permitted by the regulatory body are passed along to the consumer. Since there are no competing suppliers, there is no comparative basis upon which to assess the cost effectiveness of the utility and, consequently, the economic costs of discrimination are not easily identified. As a result, bureaucrats within a utility may indulge their tastes for discrimination without bearing the consequences.

The potential for the breakdown of natural consequence is particularly significant in the case of government departments and agencies where no profit accounting is even attempted. The decision of a government manager to make personnel selections according to racial, sexual, or ethnic criteria does not "cost" the bureaucrat anything. The fact that less productive employees are hired because of their colour or sex does lead to a lower overall productivity performance in the department or agency, but the associated costs are not identified -- and are not borne by the discriminator in question.

Anti-Jewish discrimination

An early attempt[6] to measure the impact of discriminatory behaviour in the case of regulated monopoly and other non-competitive industries discovered that Jews were much more likely to find employment in competitive industry. The study focused on MBA graduates from Harvard University and discovered that the number of Jews actually employed in the regulated monopoly sectors of the economy was less than half the number that would be expected if there were no religious discrimination on the part of employers.

Discriminators in these non-competitive situations are not provided with an incentive to change their behaviour. There is thus no reason to suppose that they will. On the other hand, in a very competitive environment, even the most diehard discriminators may have to reconsider their behaviour, because the desire to discriminate places the employer at a competitive disadvantage.

In a competitive industry, employers must constantly seek out ways to better other companies. Every avenue of cost reduction and sales promotion must be explored. Failure to respond to the continuous challenge of the market would mean eventual displacement by a more cost effective firm. Evidently, an employer who decided to hire on the basis of criteria other than those related to an employee's ability to contribute to the firm's profitability would not be able to persist for long in this behaviour, for the employer's willingness to operate under the competitive disadvantage of discrimination would confer an advantage on his or her competitors. So, even if some employers were willing to pay the price of discrimination, it is likely that the competitive process would eventually reduce their numbers or even weed them out.

A double-edged sword

The pursuit of profit works both ways on discriminatory practices, however, and some discrimination takes place precisely because the economic process rewards those who put profits first. An important instance of this is to be found in the case of consumer discrimination. Here the producers of a particular product or service do not themselves discriminate; it is rather the consumers of the product or service who do.

For example, consider restauranteurs who become aware that their patrons do not wish to be served by individuals of particular racial or ethnic backgrounds. These restauranteurs -- while not themselves wishing to discriminate -- will, nevertheless, discriminate in their hiring practices in order to please their customers and best satisfy the market they face. Of course, the discriminatory hiring practice means that the restauranteurs must charge higher prices for meals -- a cost which is borne by the discriminatory patrons.

In this case, the employers' pursuit of profit leads to discrimination -- but only on behalf of his customers. He himself is "colourblind." It is his customers who express a preference, for which they are willing to pay in the form of higher prices. Similar consumer discrimination can be observed in restaurants where patrons do not wish to dine with people of different racial or ethnic extraction. For the most part, this happens naturally in homogeneous ethnic neighbourhoods. However, to the extent that restauranteurs actually prohibit or discourage people of a certain extraction, they are again only catering to the desires of their customers -- as reflected in the higher price such meals command when served in homogeneous surroundings.

HOW MUCH DISCRIMINATION?

The starting point in any analysis of discrimination must be that, in general, people attempt to discriminate in every aspect of their lives. We have discerned, however, that the extent to which they actually will discriminate depends on how much it costs. As employers or consumers, even as employees, people must pay for their preferences, and this tends to limit the amount of discrimination. In the case of employers, the extent of discrimination will, for the most part, be limited by the force of competition. In competitive industries, the decision to discriminate may cost employers dearly, and for that reason the more competitive[7] the industry, the less likely one is to discover discriminatory hiring practices. However, not all industries are competitive (public utilities and government agencies in particular), and the discriminatory tendencies of consumers may persist even in the face of higher prices. The question naturally arises, then, as to how much discrimination exists and how much will continue to exist.

The mandate

All of this is by way of introduction to our present task. With this brief overview of the economics of discrimination, we are now ready to analyze the Abella Report.[8]

Judge Rosalie Abella of the Ontario Provincial Court (Family Division) was charged by then Minister of Employment and Immigration, Lloyd Axworthy, to study the employment practices of eleven designated Crown and other government-owned corporations regarding women, native people, disabled persons, and visible minorities.

She recommended government action to enforce equal pay for equal work (EPFEW), equal pay for work of equal value (EPFWOEV), and enhanced education and childcare facilities, all at taxpayer expense. She urged these provisions not only for the public sector she was to have studied, according to her mandate, but for the private sector as well. In addition, she suggests that these programs be compulsory for all employers, and proposes four models of enforcement: expansion of the Canadian Human Rights Commission; setting up a new independent agency; asking that the Canadian Labour Market and Productivity Centre assist the CHRC; and hiring special "labour inspectors" to monitor violations of "employment equity." (Commissioner Abella prefers to characterize her recommendations as "employment equity," rather than the more accurate "affirmative action," or the even more precise "quotas" or "reverse discrimination.")

Taken by themselves and without reference to a dispassionate analytical framework, the Abella Report recommendations have a certain appeal. However, against the background of a careful consideration of the causes of unequal representation of groups in employments, the Abella Report analysis is found wanting, its conclusions inconsistent and its recommendations repetitious of mistakes which have been made in similar programs elsewhere.

CHAPTER 2

THE METHODOLOGY OF DISCRIMINATION

Public vs. private

The first shortcoming in the Abella Report (AR, henceforth) is a failure to adequately distinguish between the public and private sectors. As we have seen, the institution of profit and loss can be a powerful barrier against the expression of discrimination in the labour market. Those who indulge such prejudices will have to pay higher salaries for a given quality of employees, or make do with workers of lesser skills at the same wage. In either case, losses in the competitive struggle will tend to ensue.

However, the profit and loss system operates only in the private sector, not the public. If there is, therefore, any case to be made for affirmative action, it is far stronger in government employment, than in the private sector.[9] At the very least, it is crucial to keep this distinction in mind in any analysis of discriminatory behaviour. But in this regard, the AR is unfortunately found wanting.

An inquiry

According to the specific Terms of Reference imposed on Judge Abella,

> it is desirable that an inquiry be made into the opportunities for employment of women, native people, disabled persons and visible minorities in certain crown corporations and corporations wholly owned by the Government of Canada. (p. ii)

To this end, Judge Abella is charged with the task of

> examining the employment practices of Petro Canada, Air Canada, Canadian National Railway Company, Canada Mortgage and Housing Corporation, Canada Post Corporation, Canadian Broadcasting Corporation, Atomic Energy of Canada Limited, Export Development Corporation, Teleglobe Canada and the de Havilland Aircraft of Canada, Limited and the Federal Business Development Bank; (p. ii) [10]

However, although admitting that,

> it was to inquire specifically into the employment practices of 11 designated crown and government-owned corporations. (p. v)

the AR, on its very first page, chafed at the bit. Yearning to be "free," the Abella Report explained its decision to transcend its limited mandate as follows:

> It was clear at the outset that only a broad approach would serve, and the Commission therefore treated the 11 designated corporations as illustrative models of the issues under study. No corporation's employment practices can be assessed fairly in a cultural vacuum. It would be difficult at best to make judgements about the adequacy of the practices of crown and government-owned corporations without placing these practices in the context of what other Canadians do, believe, or expect.
>
> Moreover, without an overall analysis of the multidimensional nature of the barriers facing the four designated groups, a distorted perspective emerges. The climate in any given corporation reflects the social, cultural, economic, and political environment in which the corporation functions. To study a corporation's employment practices, therefore, one must also study the realities of the wider community. To recommend

effective remedial measures to neutralize obstacles to equality, one must concentrate at least as intensively on the societal as on the corporate reflection of the problem.

The focus of the Commission was on matters within federal jurisdiction. However, the issues could not be so circumscribed and the organizations and individuals who met and made submissions to the Commission were not so constrained. (p. v)

This, however, will not do. The AR methodology might suffice were there no relevant differences between government and market employment. But as we have seen, there are, and they are crucially important. Consequently, it is one of the great flaws of the Abella Report that it exceeds its terms of reference and proceeds to discuss the "realities of the wider community." Because of this departure the AR prescribes compulsory legislation not only for the public sector, but for corporations doing business with government, and indeed for all employers, whether public or private. Although the Abella Report cites some of the relevant Fraser Institute research on the differing effects of discrimination in the public and private sectors in its appendix,[11] it shows no evidence of having taken it into account.

Definitions

The AR begins in Chapter 1 with an attempt to define equality in employment.

To begin with, it asserts,

Equality is thus a process - a process of constant and flexible examination, of vigilant introspection, and of aggressive open-mindedness. (p. 1)

By way of explication it maintains that,

> One hundred years ago, the role for women was almost exclusively domestic; 50 years ago, some visible minorities were disenfranchised; 25 years ago, native persons were routinely kept dependent. Today, none of these exclusionary assumptions is acceptable. (p. 1)

But equality is not a process. It is a condition. Webster's Dictionary defines the word as follows: "the state of being equal." Leaving aside exactly what equality is, for the moment, it is at least capable, in principle, of being attained one day. After that glorious occasion, no further "process" need occur. Or rather, since by stipulation we will have already arrived at equality on that day, any further activity on this front, or "process," would only erode this accomplishment.

This, of course, is not meant to deny that discovery of the truth about equality (or about anything else for that matter) is not a process. Of course it is. Human beings, at least on this side of the Garden of Eden, must always seek and struggle and examine and be vigilant and open-minded in their attempts to gain knowledge. This struggle is a process. But the thing we are attempting to learn about need not therefore itself be a process. Mankind is constantly trying to learn more about the laws which govern the physical universe. This attempt is a process. But that does not mean that the physical principles of the universe are changing. They are, rather, a set of unchanging forces capable, in principle, of being discovered.

Equity or justice on the other hand is clearly process related.[12] Equality of results may be desirable, but if that outcome is achieved by force of law, it may not be just. On the other hand, inequality arrived at by a just process would be just. This paradox lies at the very root of the debate about legislative remedies for perceived "inequality."

Fairness

What, exactly, is equality in employment?

As the learned author of a multi-million dollar report advocating employment equality,[13] it would seem incumbent on Judge Abella to provide at least a "working" answer to this perplexing problem. In the event, however, we are sorely disappointed.

States the Abella Report:

> If in this ongoing process we are not always sure what 'equality' means, most of us have a good understanding of what is 'fair.' And what is happening today in Canada to women, native people, disabled persons, and visible minorities is not fair.
>
> It is not fair that many people in these groups have restricted employment opportunities, limited access to decision-making processes that critically affect them, little public visibility as contributing Canadians, and a circumscribed range of options generally. It may be understandable, given history, culture, economics, and even human nature, but by no-standard is it fair. (p. 1)

But this is far from acceptable. If Judge Abella is not sure what "equality" means, of what use is a good understanding of "fair"? What is the supposed relationship between "equality" and "fair"? If it is one of equivalence, then lack of knowledge of the former should spill over onto the latter; if it is not, then what, pray tell, is the relevance of "fairness"?

Further, _why_ is it not fair that "many people in these groups have restricted employment opportunities"? Whose employment opportunities, after all, are completely unrestricted?

Moreover, it is only in a self-sufficiency economy that people can have "full access to decision-making processes that critically affect them." Only when each person produces for himself all the goods and services he needs, can he have full access to decision-making processes that critically affect him. But most people have chosen, for a variety of reasons,[14] to live in societies which make use of specialization, the division of labour, and trade. As such, we can at best have very limited access to these decisions, for most of them will be made by millions of people we don't even know.[15]

No standards

According to the AR, "by no standard is (any of the foregoing) fair." The problem is, no standards for fairness are put forth. Rather, an "appeal" is made "to our collective sense of fairness" (p. 2). But this is surely inexact, and subjective. How can we rely upon a collective sense of fairness as the bedrock of our analysis when this is itself so great a source of contention? For example, it might be unfair that talent, intelligence, industriousness, artistic sensibility, inventiveness, entrepreneurial ability, happy dispositions, etc., are spread as unequally as they are throughout our nation. Perhaps it would be more "fair" if these attributes were uniform over the population.[16]

But given their unequal distribution throughout the populace, it is unclear whether the resulting employment inequalities are "fair" or not. Certainly we are given no clear criterion in the AR upon which such a judgement can be made.

To be sure, there is some sense in which it is patently clear that the present distribution of say, I.Q. points is highly "unfair." ("It just isn't 'fair' that some people, through no fault of their own, are born with an I.Q. of 70.") The difficulty with putting matters in this way is that it implies that something can be done, and moreover, should be done. Suppose there were a machine that could take 40 I.Q. points from those at the 150 level, and redistribute it to those who otherwise would have had to struggle along with I.Q.s of only 70, leaving everyone exactly equal at 110 I.Q. Could we force everyone in society to take part in such a procedure? This would hardly be "fair," since justice includes the notion that it is improper to treat people in so cavalier a manner. Nor is this discussion of what is "equal," "fair," or "just" merely a matter of semantics. What is clear is that we can make no sensible comment about the fairness, equality or justice of a condition or circumstance unless we know how it has arisen.

Quotas

Next, we turn to a consideration of quotas, or proportional representation, sometimes called "reverse discrimination." There can be little doubt that legislated quota systems are unjust. They treat the individual on the basis of group membership, and are prejudicial to people such as white males,[17] who may themselves never have been guilty of any discriminatory practices. In addition, they rend the social fabric, as they set race against race, ethnic group against ethnic group, gender against gender.[18]

So historically, the demand for "quotas" was dropped from the ongoing dialogue, but not the reality. Instead, the package was relabelled, and called "timetables." But this, too, created problems, when the obvious question arose: timetables toward what? Since the answer was "quotas," and "quotas" were unsavory, timetables were renounced as well.[19]

Next into the batter's box stepped "affirmative action." This was upbeat, this was positive, this was "affirmative." It meant the same thing, of course, but no matter; it was more acceptable to the public; and this is all that counted.

You can fool some of the people all of the time, and most of the people some of the time, but eventually they begin to catch on. In just this manner, affirmative action began to lose its catchet. Says the AR:

> People generally have a sense that 'affirmative action' refers to interventionist government policies, and that is enough to prompt a negative reaction from many. (p. 7)

Because of such "misunderstanding" and "disagreements" about the phrase, and the "foreclosure" of "discussion" because of the "waving of the semantic red flag," there is yet again need of a new language. The Abella

> Commission notes this in order to propose that a new term, 'employment equity,' be adopted to describe programs of positive remedy for discrimination in the Canadian workplace. No great principle is sacrificed in exchanging phrases of disputed definition for new ones that may be more accurate and less destructive of reasoned debate.
>
> In devising their unique program, the Americans have called it affirmative action. In most people's minds, it has become associated with the imposition of quotas. In creating our own program in Canada, we may not wish to use quotas and we should therefore seriously consider calling it something else if we want to avoid some of the

intellectual resistance and confusion. It is not imperative that we do so, but it is worth considering. (p. 7)

Synonyms

This would be all well and good had Judge Abella not only eschewed the word "quotas," but the reality as well. However, and this is highly unfortunate, "employment equity" is yet another thinly disguised synonym for quotas, one in a long line of such attempts. For says the AR in its list of recommendations,

> 3. The statutory requirement to implement employment equity should oblige employers to develop and maintain employment practices designed to eliminate discriminatory barriers and <u>to improve where necessary</u> the participation of women, native people, disabled persons, and specified ethnic and racial groups in the workplace. <u>No quotas should be imposed.</u>

> 7. Since the goal of imposing a statutory obligation to implement employment equity is to expand employment opportunities of qualified individuals in the designated groups by eliminating discriminatory barriers in the workplace, <u>results, not systems</u>, should be reviewed initially.

> If the results are found to be <u>unreasonably low</u> by the enforcement agency, taking into account the employer's job openings, prior record, and the realities of the local labour force, the enforcement agency would determine whether or not the results reflect discriminatory practices. If they do, the employer would be advised to amend these practices. (emphasis added) (pp. 255, 256)

On the face of it, recommendations 3 and 7 would seem to contradict claims that the AR still relies on quotas, no matter how misguided, outmoded or rejected. Could it be more clear? "No quotas should be imposed" appears in sharp black and white in the report. Nevertheless, we maintain that the reality of the recommendations, and the way they would function were they ever implemented, would be to utilize quotas, despite the specific disavowal to the contrary. What is the evidence for this claim?

Results, not systems

Let us first consider the very wording of the AR recommendations cited above. Quotas are specifically disavowed, but AR calls for the "improvement where necessary" of the participation of women. This immediately raises the question, When will improvement be deemed necessary? What conditions will require the amelioration of law? Since it is "results, not systems" which matter, we can deduce that it will not be employment practices, but rather the failure of women (or other groups) to achieve the numerical representation in any given occupation to which their proportion of the total population would presumably entitle them.[20]

This point may be made forcibly by analogy. The Civil Rights Act of 1964 made it illegal, in the United States, to prohibit blacks from using public water fountains and restrooms. In Judge Abella's terminology, the situation was with a stroke of the pen changed from a "system" which allowed state-mandated discrimination, to one which prohibited it. But the "results" were not automatically altered; that came later, as people began to use these now-integrated facilities.

Suppose that blacks in 1965 comprised 12 percent of the population of a southern state in the U.S., but, based on a careful compilation of statistics, accounted for only 5 percent of the usage of restrooms and other such public accommodations. According to the "systems" criterion, all would be well, since blacks had as much right to use the facilities, and these rights were strictly protected. However, according to the benchmark of "results" which the AR urges upon the Canadian government, things would be seriously amiss. For the black utilization of water fountains etc., would be only roughly half the rate one might anticipate on the basis of their representation in the overall population.[21]

Process or results

With the best will in the world -- and we have no reason to credit Judge Abella with anything less than that -- one can either couch equality in employment legislation in terms of process or in terms of results. The trouble with process, from the point of view of egalitarians, is that no matter how pure and discrimination-free is the hiring process, inequality of results may -- and probably will -- still ensue, due to basic differences in people. And, the difficulty with determining freedom from discrimination on the basis of results is that this is based, essentially, on a numerical criterion. The only way for governments to ascertain whether or not discrimination has taken place is by comparing occupational status with population characteristics -- i.e., the use of the quota system.

There is additional evidence, scattered all throughout the AR, that "timetables," "affirmative action," and "employment equity" are all reducible to quotas.

Consider the following:

> In engineering and architecture, women were <u>barely represented</u>, accounting for slightly under six per cent of these occupations (8,000 females and 135,000 males). The only branch of the engineering profession with 1,000 or more women was industrial engineering. The number of women working as mathematicians, statisticians, actuaries, and other related occupations was <u>only</u> 2,000. The situation was <u>better</u> in the computer-related occupations, such as systems analysis and computer programming, which showed the greatest growth in the professional female occupations and one of the <u>lowest</u> male-female earning differentials. (emphasis added) (p. 66)

Representation

Quotas, equality of retrospective results, proportional representation, targets, are implied by the statement that women are "barely represented" in engineering and architecture. Proper representation, one can only conclude, would be more equal, or at least more equal representation than that which actually obtains. The situation is "better" in

computer-related occupations, only because the representation is more nearly equal there -- not because there is any allegation of more out and out discriminatory practices in architecture and engineering than in computers.[22]
Continues the AR:

> On the other hand, the 1970s also opened employment opportunities in systems analysis, computer programming, and related occupations - jobs requiring higher levels of skills in the utilization of computers. But in 1981 women accounted for only 29 per cent of this occupational category. Thus, although computers have opened new employment opportunities for both men and women, the employment patterns of 1981 suggest that women in the computer field may be shifting into segregated, low-paying occupations. (emphasis added) (p. 69)

It seems, however, that while the situation is "better" in computers, it is not better by nearly enough. Women account for "only" 29 per cent. Again, such an allegation is compatible, even understandable, only against a presumption of numerical representation targets or quotas. Were the target representation mentality missing, the numbers themselves, the "results," could not possibly constitute evidence of any difficulty. They could only serve to indicate that discrimination might be occurring. The numbers, that is, could be interpreted as a cautionary device. Then, the hard work of ferreting out discriminatory practices would have to begin. But in these cases, the AR is ready to use perjorative terminology ("barely," "better," "only") on the basis of only the number themselves.

The statistical record

Next, consider another bit of evidence:

> Whatever advances have been made, the 11 corporations still have far to go providing equal employment opportunities for women. The female participation rate in categories offering the greatest economic opportunities in 1983 was generally low.

The male representation in those categories was:

- 96.3 per cent male in upper-level management;
- 89.5 per cent male in middle management;
- 92.1 per cent male in professional occupations;
- 83.5 per cent male in semi-professional and technical occupations;
- 59.7 per cent male in supervisory (clerical, sales, and service) positions.

This does not represent a significant change from the male representation in 1978. (emphasis added) (pp. 109-112)

Again there is the use of pejoratives ("far to go," "low," "representation") based solely on the numerical record, without even a shred of an indication that these 11 Crown corporations were engaging in a pattern of discrimination. The numbers, as reported by the AR, are consistent with discriminatory practices. They are also consistent with non-discrimination. Were they only an indication that a discriminatory hiring and promotion policy might be occurring, further evidence must be adduced to show this. Since no pretence has even been made in the AR of claiming that actual discrimination is taking place (apart from the unequal retrospective results) we must again conclude that its underlying premise is one of numerical quotas.

Systemic discrimination

There is another indication that concern with quotas underlies the entire AR. This is its concern with "systemic discrimination." This phenomenon is defined as follows:

... the systemic approach identifies discrimination in the workplace in terms of the impact of employment practices on the employment opportunities of designated group members. The impact, rather than the intention behind behaviour or employment practices, is what defines systemic discrimination. (p. 193)

Intentions, to be sure, are not amenable to an approach which places great reliance on numerical quotas. For the intentions can succeed, or not, depending on other factors. But the impact can only be measured numerically. Thus the question of quotas must necessarily arise. Otherwise, how are we to judge any given numerical impact as (systemically) discriminatory or not? Without the quota as a benchmark or threshold, all the numbers amassed throughout the AR are just that: numbers. They are statistics from which no public policy recommendations follow, whatsoever. Only when quotas are employed, implicitly or explicitly, does it make sense to cite the statistics of female labour force experience.

If it is certain that the AR supports the quota system (despite its denials) it is no less sure that this policy has serious drawbacks. Quotas tend to harm highly competent women, by making it appear that their accomplishments are not due to their own efforts, but to government "largesse"; they harm unqualifed women by placing them in positions which expose their incompetence; they harm women excluded from affirmative action, by increasing their frustration and lowering their motivation to attain job qualifications on their own; as well, quotas exacerbate inter group animosity.[23]

CHAPTER 3

THE ECONOMICS OF DISCRIMINATION

Equal representation

We turn now to the economic predisposition which underlies the AR: that were we to live in a discrimination-free nation, all groups -- such as women, native people, disabled persons, and visible minorities -- would attain a proportionate share of all occupations, at all wage levels.[24] On a more general level, this philosophy posits that all people are basically alike, and that any actual differences can be attributed to a disturbance to this natural order -- i.e., discrimination.

The entire Chapter 2 of the AR can be seen in this light. It consists of a statistical profile of women and the other designated groups (native people, disabled persons, visible minorities) which makes little sense except as a backdrop against this theory. Why, for example, cite male-female comparisons for labour force participation rates, (Tables 2, 3, 4 and 15), occupational composition (Tables 5, 6, 7, 8 and 9), income (Tables 10, 11), union membership (Table 12), unemployment (Tables 13, 14, 16), immigrant status (Table 17) as implicit evidence of discrimination were there no tacit premise that absent this practice, the male and female statistics would be equal?

Discriminatory reality

But have we misinterpreted the AR? Is it really true that Judge Abella infers discriminatory behaviour from differential lifestyle, employment or salary results?

It is not a question of whether this discrimination is motivated by an intentional desire to obstruct someone's potential, or whether it is the accidental by-product of innocently motivated practices or systems. If the barrier is affecting certain groups in a disproportionately negative way, it is a signal that the practices that lead to this adverse impact may be discriminatory.

This is why it is important to look at the results of a system. In these results one may find evidence that barriers which are inequitable impede individual opportunity. These results are by no means conclusive evidence of inequity, but they are an effective signal that further examination is warranted to determine whether the disproportionately negative impact is in fact the result of inequitable practices, and therefore calls for remedial attention, or whether it is a reflection of a non-discriminatory reality. (pp. 2, 3)

Here, it is clearly stated that unequal "results are by no means conclusive evidence of inequity." Rather, "they are an effective signal that further examination is warranted." So it would appear that our interpretation is incorrect.

Inequity?

But there is a difficulty with any such conclusion. Suppose that in a particular case there are unequal results. We do not immediately conclude that inequity is afoot, but only engage in further research, seeking to uncover the existence of "inequitable practices." If none can be shown to exist, we conclude, presumably, that the initial unequal results, which "signaled" to us, were merely a "reflection of a non-discriminatory reality." The implicit assumption, here, is that if the inequality is a reflection of "non-discriminatory reality," then no further affirmative action policies need be implemented.

This is a crucial point, addressing perhaps the most important question in the entire AR. If Judge Abella were serious about the view that all inequality of wages is not necessarily linked to discrimination, then she would be careful to distinguish between discriminatory activity which leads to unequal wages, and non-discriminatory behaviour, which also is consistant with such a result. She is on record as stating that only the former, but not the latter, should be subjected to affirmative action legislation. One would expect pages and pages of clarification, even a whole chapter, perhaps, devoted to a delineation between these two phenomena.[25]

In the event, however, all such expectations are rudely disappointed. Apart from that one sentence on the topic quoted above, there is not a single solitary mention of the distinction between sexist behaviour and a "non-discriminatory reality."

OVERSIGHT

This being the case, we shall have to make good on this oversight. What type of behaviour, then, might be characterized as non-discriminatory reality? What situations, that is, might bring about unequal pay between the sexes, in the complete absence of all discriminatory activity whatsoever?

Biology

First is the biological fact that women, not men, become pregnant and bear children, and that this usually necessitates separation from the labour force, sometimes temporarily (a few months) and sometimes for long periods of time (several years or even decades).

Says Thomas Sowell in this regard:

> Historically, women's position relative to that of men declined for more than two decades, across a broad front, from peaks reached in the 1930s or earlier. Women's share of doctoral degrees - both Ph.D.s and M.D.s - declined, along with their representation on college and university faculties (including the faculties of women's colleges run by women administrators), as did their representation among people listed in Who's Who. Women's income as a percentage of men's income declined over a twenty year period from 1949 to 1969. If sex discrimination is the chief explanation

of the male-female economic differences, it is hard to imagine why there would have been increasing sex discrimination during this particular period of apparent female economic retrogression. However, it is much easier to understand as a consequence of a parallel decline in the age of marriage for educated women and a rising number of children per woman.[26]

Recent Canadian experience would appear to be roughly comparable to that of the U.S. In this country, too, female-male income ratios are, at least in the last two decades, highly correlated (negatively) with the birth rate. (See Tables Ia and Ib and Graphs Ia and Ib.)

Sociology

Second is the sociological fact that women bear a disproportionate share of childrearing and housekeeping responsibilities.
Continues Sowell:

> This mundane demographic explanation of socioeconomic trends also accords with recent upswings in women's occupational position as marriage and childbearing trends began to reverse in the 1960s. The same explanation is even more dramatically apparent in contemporaneous comparisons. As of 1971, single women in their thirties who had worked continuously since leaving school earned slightly more than single men of the same age, even though women as a group earned less than half as much as men as a group. In the academic world, single female faculty members who had received their Ph.D.s in the 1930s had by the 1950s become full professors to a slightly greater extent than male Ph.D.s of the same vintage, even though female academics as a group were far less successful than males by various indices. A more recent study shows that female academics who never married earned more than male academics who never married, even before 'affirmative action' 'goals and timetables' became

Table Ia

Average Female Income as a Percentage of Average Male Income

	1961	1971	1981
All Persons	41.3	44.1	49.7

Source: 1981 Census, publication #92928, table 5; 1971 Census, publication #94760, table 1, pp. 1-1,1-2; 1961 Census, Volume 4.1, tables A2, A6, pp. A2-1, A2-2, A6-1, A6-2; Fraser Institute calculations.

Table Ib

Births per 1000 Population

1981	15.3
1976	15.7
1971	16.8
1966	19.4
1961	26.1

Source: Historical Statistics of Canada, Second Edition, Series B1-14; Statistics Canada, 84-204, Vital Statistics, Vol. 1, Births and Deaths, 1983.

Graph Ia

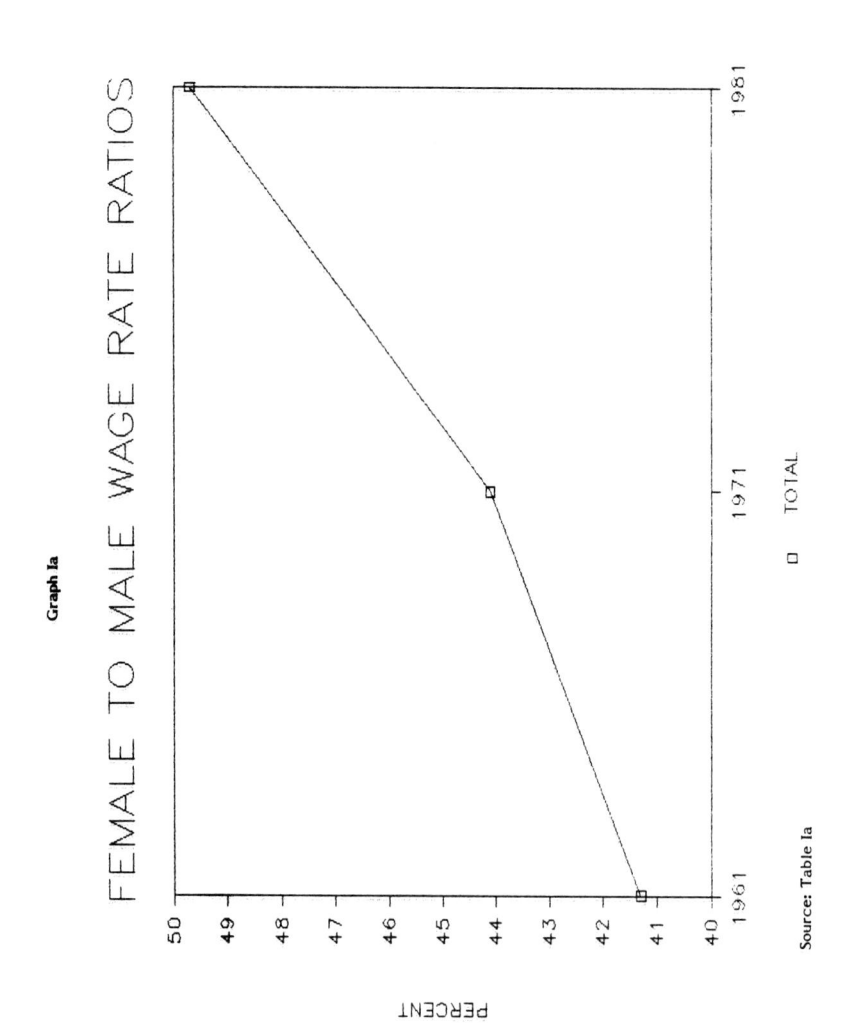

FEMALE TO MALE WAGE RATE RATIOS

PERCENT

□ TOTAL

Source: Table Ia

Graph Ib

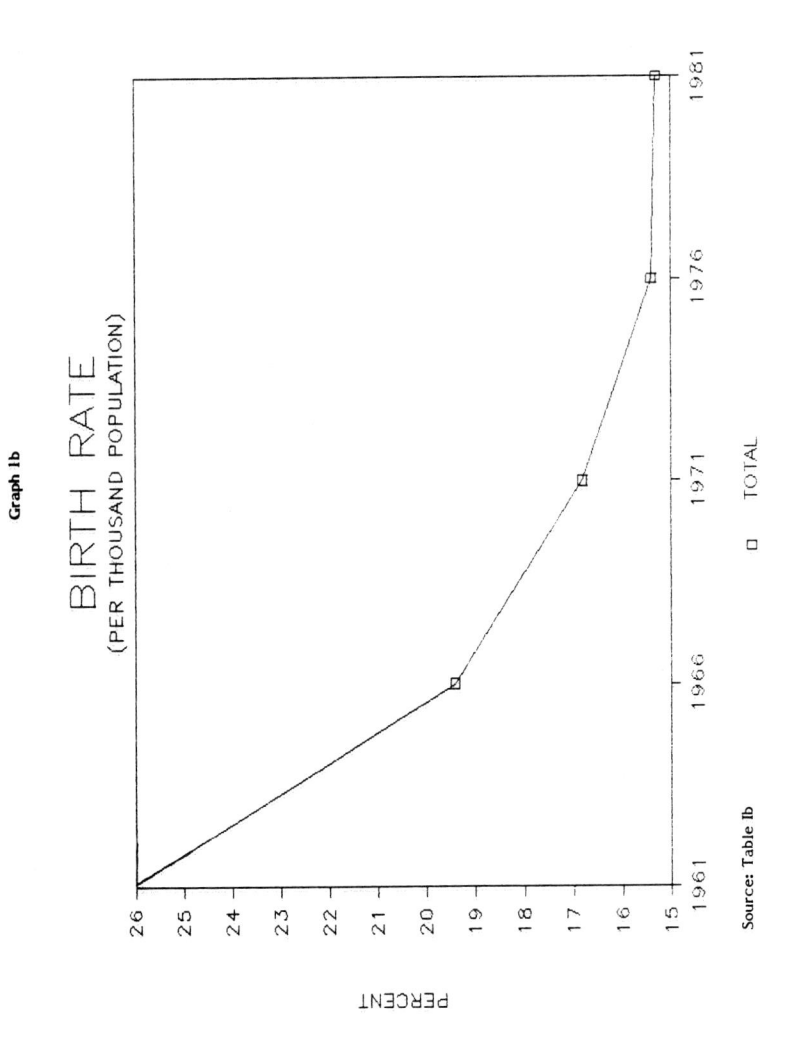

BIRTH RATE
(PER THOUSAND POPULATION)

PERCENT

26, 25, 24, 23, 22, 21, 20, 19, 18, 17, 16, 15

1961, 1966, 1971, 1976, 1981

□ TOTAL

Source: Table Ib

mandatory in 1971. Many statistical comparisons sidestep the crucial effect of marriage on women's careers in various ways, including defining 'single' women to include women who are widowed, divorced, or separated. Obviously, a woman who re-enters the labour force after many years as a housewife is unlikely to earn as much as a man who has been working continuously.[27]

The AR has not completely neglected to consider these points. On the contrary, it states:

> The problem is one of assumptions, almost religiously held, about the role and ability of women in Canada. Many men and women seem unable to escape from the perceptual fallout of the tradition that expects women to behave dependently and supportively toward men. (p. 25)

> Notwithstanding that there is an equal right to work, there is no avoiding certain biological imperatives. Women rather than men become pregnant. Children require care. An environment must therefore be created that permits the adequate care of children while also allowing the equal right of men and women to maximize their economic potential. This environment, however, is not possible if <u>the public continues to assume that the primary responsibility for the care of children belongs to women.</u> There is no mysterious chemistry that produces in one gender an enhanced ability either to raise children or to work at a paid job.

> The care of children needs to be seen as a parental rather than a maternal responsibility. We are unfairly overburdening and restricting both men and women if we fail to base practices, employment and otherwise, on a policy of shared responsibility between men and women for the care of their children. Because responsibility for childcare used to be an exclusively maternal one, the greatest psychological pressure for the care of children is still felt by women. (p. 28)

But this reply is only tangential; it fails to come directly to grips with the issue. Judge Abella as much as admits that this state of affairs is not due to employer discrimination. Rather, the explanation for the female-male wage gap is that "the public continues to assume that the primary responsibility for the care of children belongs to women." All the analysis amounts to, then, is an exhortation to the public. In effect, the AR calls for a radical restructuring of society; it counsels that men and women change their traditional ways of dealing with each other in the home, and too, their age old patterns of relating to their children.

Specialization

But there are economic reasons why the division of labour exists, why husbands tend to be more heavily oriented toward the marketplace, and wives toward home, hearth and childraising. In many cases this makes economic sense. Specialization, trade, and the division of labour are categories which apply to the household, no less than to other areas of economic life. Family income can in many cases be enhanced by only one partner working, and the other taking on the role of support staff. That the former is usually the male, and the latter the female, is of course due to social, historical, biological and cultural antecedents.

Without meaning to justify or condone the status quo in any way, both those who applaud differing sex roles, and those who oppose them, can agree that for better or worse, it will be difficult to change. Even the AR itself states "it will likely be generations before the impact of this newly sanctioned approach to marriage (one of greater equality) is reflected in society's other institutions." (p. 26) This is strong evidence that the AR in fact accepts the male-female earnings "gap" as not being due to employer discrimination -- whether "systemic," purposeful, or accidental -- but rather to the fundamental features of society -- the "non-discriminatory reality."

Most advocates of change assume that cracks are already appearing in the edifice of traditional sex roles. But there is a danger in over-estimating the importance of these fissures, for recent evidence shows little indication of basic change. Yes, labour force participation of women has been on the increase,[28] but the economic cultural and sociological underpinnings of sex role differentiation are still very much in operation.

One indication is the massive study of 6,000 couples living in the U.S., undertaken by University of Washington sociologists Philip Blumstein and Pepper Schwartz.[29] According to a Newsweek review of this book: [30]

> To their surprise, the sociologists discovered that the social and economic gains won by so many American women during the past decade have had remarkably little impact on the traditional gender roles assumed by the more than 3,600 married couples in their study. Although 60 percent of the wives had jobs, only about 30 percent of the husbands believed both spouses should work - and only 39 percent of wives thought so. No matter how large their paycheck, the working wives were still almost entirely responsible for the couple's housework. Husbands so hated housework, the researcher found, that wives who asked them to help out could sometimes sour the marriage. Most women, on the other hand -- even executives -- did not consider housework demeaning.

Traditional roles

But we need not seek far afield for evidence that traditional sex roles are very far from disappearing. The AR itself furnishes us with ample evidence on this score. For example, states this report:

> Women continue to receive most of their diplomas in the traditional areas of business secretariat, education, nursing and medical technology, community and social services, while they receive very few in the electronics and engineering areas. (p. 139)

Moreover, an examination of Tables 2 and 3 (pp. 140, 141) shows that while women have increased their percentage of first professional degrees in several areas, this "progress" is scant in some callings, and non-existent in others. Comparing the years 1972 and 1982, the female percentage rose significantly in the traditionally male areas of biology (32.8 percent to 46.4 percent), veterinary medicine (10.8 percent to 44.6 percent), dental studies (6.8 percent to 20.5 percent), architecture (9.2 percent to 24.7 percent), economics (11.2 percent to 28.4 percent), commerce (10.3 percent to 34.2 percent), law (13.9 percent to 37.6 percent), and forestry (11.5 percent to 20.7 percent). However, women are still overwhelmingly represented in household science (97.0 percent), education (73.5 percent), secretarial (99.7 percent), nursing (97.1 percent), and social work (78.0 percent). And in several hard sciences, there has been little or no change over the decade; women's share of degrees increased from 30.1 percent to 30.9 percent in mathematics, 9.8 percent to 11.5 percent in physics and 20.8 percent to 29.7 percent in chemistry. Some movement, to be sure, but hardly a revolutionary shift, not likely to create a tidal wave in male-female occupational patterns.

As well, states the AR:

> The influence of role models is subtle but often decisive. For example, there are few women in Canada in science and engineering. When one considers that, as recently as the mid-1970's guidance counsellors were reluctant to advise girls to enter careers in math-related areas or the sciences, this paucity of women is not surprising. (pp. 133, 134)

In the light of all this evidence, is it not perverse to consider the wage gap as a function of male sexist discrimination, rather than the differences of early child socialization for boys and girls?[31]

Asymmetry

A third aspect of the non-discriminatory reality is the asymmetrical effect of marriage on male and female incomes, enhancing the former, and reducing the latter. So powerful is this asymmetrical effect that the female-male earnings ratio for people who have never been married is .831, while the figure for those who have been and are married (married, divorced, widowed, separated) is .439.[32]

Some evidence for the asymmetrical effect of marriage on incomes can be found in the AR itself. For instance, Table 3 (pp. 58, 59) relates labour force participation rates for gender by marital status. First, let us compare the average labour force participation rates for all the years given (1966, 1971, 1976, 1981, 1982) between married and single women. The married women's rate is 40.86 percent, while the single women's rate is 59.04 percent, fully 18.18 percentage points higher. This illustrates the contention that marriage reduces the adherence to the marketplace on the part of women. In contrast, the married male labour force participation rate is 85.06 percent, fully 18.60 percentage points higher than that of single men, which is 66.46 percent. This is entirely compatible with our view that the institution of marriage increases male participation in the labour market.

Refuseniks

A fourth cause of male-female income differences, apart from employer discrimination, is the phenomenon of women refusing promotions or wage increases which would raise their incomes above those of their husbands or boyfriends. They do so, moreover, out of fear that such behaviour would threaten these relationships, which they evidently regard as more important than the pay hikes.

If such behaviour occurs regularly, or even to some slight but significant degree, it can certainly account for a female-male wage ratio of less than unity, in the complete absence of employer discrimination. And, like it or not, no matter how repugnant it may be to some people, there is evidence that this phenomenon actually does take place. For example, according to Jesse Bernard, there is "a determined effort, on the part of academic women not to outshine (their) husbands."[33] Vivian Gornick comments on the typical response of a woman who "deliberately lower(s) her academic standing... while she does all she subtly can to help (her future husband)."[34] Dorothy Jongeward and Dru Scott report the following wife's statement as typical:

> I would never take a job where I earned more than (my husband). If I start being really successful, that means I'm making him less of a man.[35]

Relocation

There is a fifth aspect as well. This is the fact that married men regard their jobs as much more important than do married women who are employed. One element in this phenomenon is that an employed couple is far more likely to relocate if the husband receives a better job offer elsewhere, even if the wife has few opportunities in the new locale, than if the reverse pertains.

As can be seen in Table II, only 4 percent of men, but 53 percent of women would give up their present job if their spouse's career required a move to a new geographical location. Moreover, 92 percent of husbands, and only 55 percent of wives, expected their spouses to agree to such a move to enhance their careers.

Table II

	Men	Women
Would give up XYZ job if spouse's job required a move	4%	53%
Spouse would give up job if respondent's job required a move	92%	55%
Respondent's job more important to family than spouse's	90%	34%
Spouse's job more important	4%	50%
Respondent's job primary (see text)	78%	22%
Mixed, intermediate	22%	57%
Respondent's job secondary	0%	21%

Source: Carl Hoffman and John Reed, "When Is Imbalance Not Discrimination?" Discrimination, Affirmative Action, and Equal Opportunity, op. cit., p. 201.

CHAPTER 4

A STATISTICAL ANALYSIS OF DISCRIMINATION

Interpretation

In the last chapter we saw that a difficulty with the AR is that it ignores five aspects of a non-discriminatory reality. It allows no role, that is, for biological or social factors, it fails to come to grips with the asymmetrical effects of marriage on male and female incomes, it evades the fact married women, but not men, sometimes refuse wage increases and promotions, and that relocation decisions overwhelmingly favour the married man, not his employed wife. Instead, the AR attributes all male-female income disparities to employer discrimination. The present chapter subjects the two alternative hypotheses (employer discrimination, a "non-discriminatory reality" as explanations for the male-female earnings gap) to a barrage of statistical tests. In this regard, it is an interesting exercise to contrast our Table III with Table 10 of the AR, repeated below, with additions, as Table IV.

Based on Table IV, one might surmise that over the 12 year span covered, discrimination was alive and well in Canada, although its effects have been very slightly moderated, particularly between 1977 and 1979. If we adopt the convention that absent all employer discrimination, average female employment income as a percentage of average male employment income would have been 100 percent for all the years in question, then we may say that the "discrimination rate" (100 percent minus the actual ratio) was

Table III

Average Female Income as a Percentage of

Average Male Income ("Discrimination" Rate)

	1941		1951		1961		1971		1981	
Never Married Persons	80.7	(19.3)	82.6	(17.4)	90.0	(10.0)	88.2	(11.8)	83.1	(16.9)
Ever Married Persons (married, widowed, divorced, separated)	41.3	(58.7)	46.1	(53.9)	34.2	(65.8)	37.5	(62.5)	43.9	(56.1)
All Persons	49.3	(50.7)	53.8	(46.2)	41.3	(58.7)	44.1	(55.9)	49.7	(50.3)

Source: 1981 Census, publication #92928, table 5; 1971 Census, publication #94760, table 1, pp. 1-1, 1-2; 1961 Census, Volume 4.1, tables A2, A6, pp. A2-1, A2-2, A6-1, A6-2; 1951 Census, Vol. V, table 17; 1941 Census, vol. VI, table 5; Fraser Institute calculations.

The "Discrimination" Rate, which appears in parenthesis is computed by subtracting from 1.0 the ratio of female to male income.

Table IV

Year	Average Female Employment Income as a Percentage of Average Male Employment Income	"Discrimination Rate" %
(1)	(2)	(3)
1971	60.5	39.5
1973	60.1	39.5
1975	61.0	39.0
1977	61.7	38.3
1979	63.3	36.7
1981	63.5	36.5
1982	63.9	36.1

Source: Statistics Canada. Surveys of Consumer Finances.

a. Columns (1) and (2) appear in the AR, p. 73.
b. Column (3) is computed by subtracting Column (2) from 100%.

Graph II

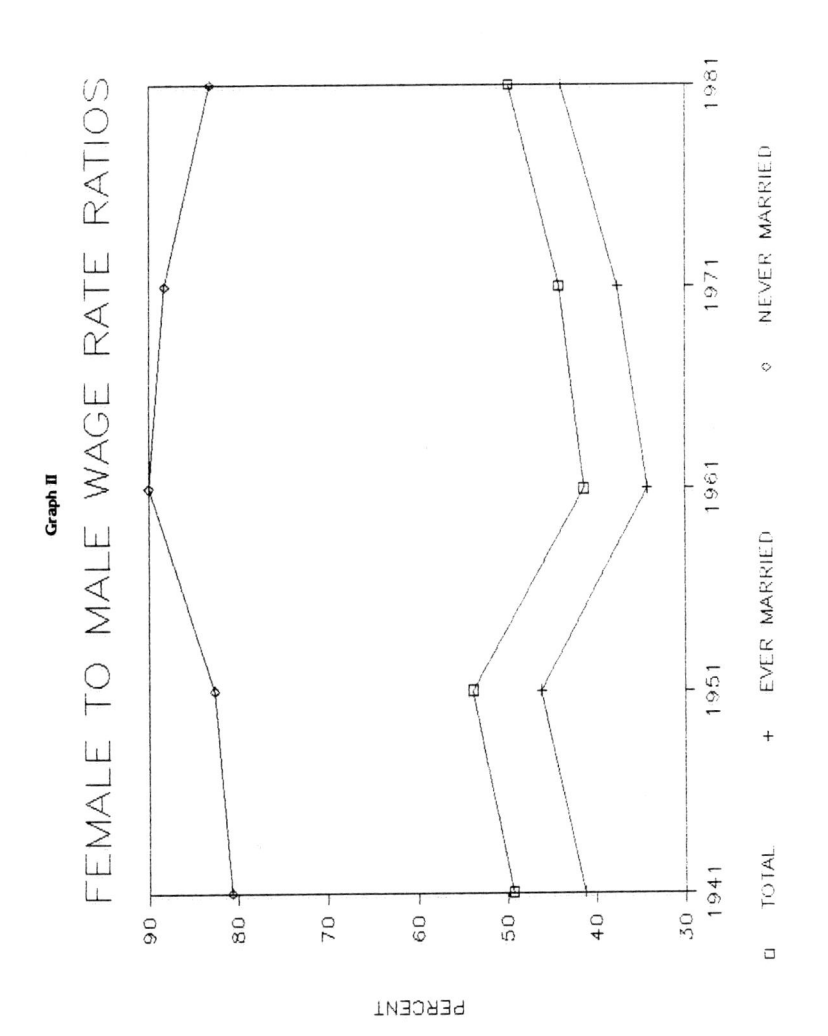

FEMALE TO MALE WAGE RATE RATIOS

□ TOTAL + EVER MARRIED ◇ NEVER MARRIED

an alarming and sexist 39.5 percent in 1971, and fell, but only to 36.1 percent, in 1982. This would be a decrease in discrimination, to be sure, but nothing upon which to base the conclusion that "women have come a long way, baby."

However, a perusal of Table III and Graph II tells a far different story. Here, the data is adjusted for marital status. Were we for the moment to ignore this refinement, we might be tempted to draw the same implications as did the AR. That is, considering for the moment only the 1961 - 1981 experience for all persons (row 3, Table III, middle curve, Graph II), and/or for ever-married persons (row 2, Table III, lowest curve, Graph II), we might well again conclude, with the AR, that sexual discrimination in Canada is rampant, but that its incidence had been declining somewhat in the last two decades.[36]

A glance at the data for never-married persons (row 1, Table III, highest curve, Graph II), however, throws cold water at this AR hypothesis. A superficial perusal of this information would appear to indicate that sexual discrimination is not as serious as thought (for example, a "discrimination rate" of 10 percent in 1961 is far lower than any reported by the AR), but that it is increasing! That is, employers in 1981 were actually more sexist, not less, than in 1961.

Marital status

The real paradox, however, arises when we consider not the rows of Table III, but the columns (or compare the curves in Graph II). Take 1961 for example. This information is impossible to reconcile with the AR employer discrimination hypothesis. Why, in this view, would there be such a gigantic difference in the female-male income ratios between never and ever-married persons? The "discrimination ratio" is only 10.0 percent for those who have not been personally touched by the institution of marriage, whereas for the married, widowed, divorced and separated, the "discrimination ratio" is a whopping 65.8 percent, some five and a half times higher. Do sexist employers discriminate heavily against ever-married women, but hardly at all against single females? Nonsense. If anything, according to the philosophy that permeates the AR, the vituperation of the typical discriminating white male employer might be expected to be concentrated on single women. For are not they in violation of the chauvenist's fervent desire to see all women "barefoot, pregnant and in the kitchen," and presumably married? As well, never-married women might be seen as a challenge to the "sexist" institution of the family, at least in the way some people view the prejudiced male employer. If so, then we would expect discrimination against all women, to be sure, but focused against never-married females. The facts of the case, however, indicate the very opposite.

It is easy to see that the employer discrimination hypothesis is untenable. In contrast, the marriage asymmetry hypothesis[37] need not go through any such convolutions to explain the facts. Indeed, they are entirely consistent with this view, showing that marriage increases the recorded earnings of married males, in contrast both to unmarried men (husbands have a helper denied to bachelors) and to married women (who take on the economic function of enhancing the income misleadingly credited to the husband alone).

A half century

Now let us consider the data for the past five decades (see Graph II). Several things become clear from this graphical summary of the statistics. First of all, it is clear that the female-male earnings ratio for all Canadians closely parallels the one for ever-married members of our society. This is no accident, but rather flows from the fact that a large proportion of employed adult Canadians are either married now, or have been married in the past.[38] The second brute fact which confronts us is that the never-married female-male earnings ratio is, roughly speaking, just about twice as great as that for the ever-marrieds. This finding is incompatible with employer discrimination as an explanation of the gap, as we have seen.

Thirdly, we must be cognizant of the fact that the female-male income ratio has never fallen below 80 percent in the past 50 years, and has reached the 90 percent level in 1961. This is truly a startling occurrence, given the widespread notion that women have been victimized by employer discrimination, and the popular conception that a female-male earnings gap of some 40 percent can be explained in terms of such discrimination. When we reflect that these data describe the work experience of all Canadians, and have not been adjusted for anything, except marital status, these findings appear almost counterintuitive. Nevertheless, were they corrected for age, education, weeks worked per year, full-time and part-time status,[39] to say nothing of occupational status, degree of unionization, uninterrupted years in the labour force, there is little doubt that the female-male income ratio would approach 100 percent, i.e., that the "gap" would vanish entirely.[40]

Variability

A fourth point which becomes apparent from a perusal of this data is that the female-male earnings ratio has been highly variable over the past five decades. For the never-marrieds, it posted an 80.7 percent mark in 1941, moved up slightly to 82.6 percent in 1951, jumped to 90.0 percent in 1961, and then fell to 88.2 percent in 1971, and to 83.1 percent in 1981. For the ever-marrieds, it registered in at the 41.3 percent level in 1941, moved up briskly to 46.1 percent in 1951, plummeted sharply to a 50 year low of 34.2 percent in 1961 (a fall of almost 12 percentage points), rose to 37.5 percent in 1971, and jumped again to 43.9 percent in 1981.[41]
The causes for these complex occurrences must be many and varied, and perhaps worthy of an entire study of their own. But whatever the ultimate explanations, one thing is clear: employer discrimination can play at best only a very minor and marginal role in our understanding of this phenomenon.[42] For in the last 40 years, whenever the ratio for ever-marrieds rose, the ratio for never-marrieds fell (1961-1981); and whenever the ratio for ever-marrieds decreased, the ratio for never-marrieds increased (1951-1961). It is only in the decade 1941-1951 that the two ratios moved in step with each other. But here, contrary to the usual expectations, both female-male ratios posted gains, seemingly, and counterintuitively, based on the "sexist" hypothesis, indicating a decline in employer discrimination against women.[43]

Globe and Mail

The AR is not the only document which egregiously overlooks the importance of marital status for male-female income comparisons. The publications of some of the most prestigious institutions in Canada are also guilty of this oversight. The <u>Globe and Mail</u> commits this sin of omission, and with a vengeance. In a page one, top of the page headline, in 36 point, ultra bold type face, positively dripping black ink, it screams "Educated women victims of wage gap, Statscan says."[44] And its story goes on to cite evidence in behalf of this claim:

- Canadian women with university degrees earn just $1,600 more a year than men with high school education.

- ... working women who graduated from university earn just $4,000 more annually than men with less than Grade 9 schooling.

- female (university) graduates earn about one-third less than male graduates.

- In 1982, a woman with a university degree averaged $24,380 in earnings, compared with $36,270 for a male university graduate, $22,800 for a man who finished high school and $20,000 for a man with elementary schooling.

- In 1982, a woman working full-time earned about $16,000 -- or $9,000 less than the average wage of a working man.

On the basis of these statistics, the Globe and Mail quoted Ottawa economist Monica Townson who parroted the AR philosophy. She opined that "jobs held by women are valued less than those held by men, which accounts for the wage gap," and recommended the passage of remedial legislation to help the "victims" of the "wage gap." Worse, this newspaper story juxtaposed data on rape implying that Canadian women are being victimized in more than one way from the same underlying cause.

StatsCan

In its story, the Globe and Mail cited a report published by Statistics Canada as the source of this information on male and female wages. The relevant part of this report, Women in Canada[45] is reproduced below as Table V. As can be seen, apart from rounding errors, the Globe and Mail story is an

Table V

Average Annual Earnings of Full-time Workers by Educational Attainment, 1971 and 1982

Earnings of Full-Time Workers[1]

	1971			1982		
	Women	Men	Women's Earnings as a % of Men's	Women	Men	Women's Earnings as a % of Men's
	$	$		$	$	
Educational Attainment						
Less than grade 9	3,732	6,722	55.5	11,804	20,073	58.8
High school[2]	4,734	8,332	56.8	14,087	22,778	61.8
Some post secondary	5,903	9,955	59.3	16,577	24,662	67.2
Post secondary certificate or diploma	6,569	9,813	66.9	17,607	26,123	67.4
University degree	9,541	15,589	61.2	24,380	36,266	67.2
Total	5,232	8,770	59.7	16,056	25,096	64.0

[1] A full-time worker is a person who worked, mostly full-time, 50-52 weeks in 1971 and 49-52 weeks in 1982.
[2] Includes persons who have either completed or attended high school.

Source: <u>Women in Canada: A Statistical Report</u>, Ottawa, Statistics Canada 1985, Cat. No. 89-503E, table 13, p. 40; **Earnings of Men and Women,** Statistics Canada Catalogue 13-577.

accurate representation of the StatsCan material. And, indeed, with this sort of data, it is entirely understandable why the Globe and Mail journalist should conclude that educated women in Canada are being "victimized" with regard to wages.

However, when marital status is incorporated into the analysis (see Tables VI and VII), the statistics tell an entirely different story. (This material was never published by Statistics Canada. Rather, it was compiled by StatsCan from the same survey material under a special contract with the Fraser Institute. This was a costly operation for the impecunious Fraser Institute but it was felt important to acquaint the public with the true facts -- which otherwise would never have seen the light of day.)

Yes, all women with a university degree earn $24,380, and all men with a high school diploma earn $22,778, and this is only $1,602 more. And married university women ($24,394) do even worse: they take home only $264 more than do married male high school graduates ($24,130). But, in very stark contrast indeed, <u>unmarried</u> female university graduates have it all over their unmarried male counterparts with only high school education; the women post an average income of $24,349. while the men earn only $16,201 -- a differential of slightly over 50 percent. So education does matter -- when marital status is taken into account.

The story behind the story

It is the same story with the comparison between university-educated women and men with less than 9 years of schooling. To be sure, all such women ($24,380) have only a slight ($4,307) remuneration advantage over all such men ($20,073). And married females ($24,394) again do even worse, as we would expect, registering an even smaller superiority ($3,664) over married males ($20,730). But as in the previous example, this pattern does not at all hold for the comparison between <u>never-married</u> university women, and <u>never-married</u> grade school men. Here, the females earn $24,349, the males $12,089, for a gap of $12,260, an amount larger than the total income of the men!

Next, consider the Globe and Mail claim that "In 1982, a woman working full-time earned about $16,000 -- or $9,000 less than the average wage of a working man." Actually, the shortfall was $9,040, or 36.0 percent, the difference between

Table VI

Average Annual Earnings of Full-time Workers by Educational Attainment and Marital Status = Other, 1971 and 1982

Other

(incl. married, divorced, widowed)

Earnings of Full-time Workers[1]

	1971			1982		
	Women	Men	Women's Earnings as a % of Men's	Women	Men	Women's Earnings as a % of Men's
Educational Attainment						
Less than grade 9	3,847	6,928	55.5	12,001	20,730	57.9
High school[2]	4,891	8,722	56.1	14,269	24,130	59.1
Some post-secondary	6,027	10,529	57.2	16,872	26,289	64.2
Post-secondary certificate or diploma	6,707	10,143	66.1	17,542	27,476	63.8
University degree	9,432	16,606	56.8	24,394	37,881	64.4
Total	5,289	9,147	57.8	15,973	26,362	60.6

[1] A full-time worker is a person who worked, mostly full-time, 50-52 weeks in 1971 and 49-52 weeks in 1982.

[2] Includes persons who have either completed or attended high school.

Source: Survey of Consumer Finances - 1972-1983, Unpublished Data. These data are herein published with the authorization of the Director, Household Survey Division.

Table VII

Average Annual Earnings of Full-time Workers by Educational Attainment and Marital Status = Single, 1971 and 1982

Single
(Never Married)

Earnings of Full-time Workers[1]

	1971 Women $	1971 Men $	Women's Earnings as a % of Men's	1982 Women $	1982 Men $	Women's Earnings as a % of Men's
Educational Attainment						
Less than grade 9	3,265	4,624	70.6	10,302	12,089	85.2
High School[2]	4,369	5,712	76.5	13,436	16,201	82.9
Some post-secondary	5,652	6,442	87.7	15,957	18,905	84.4
Post-secondary certificate or diploma	6,277	7,008	89.6	17,784	19,045	93.4
University degree	9,720	8,855	109.8	24,349	26,679	91.3
Total	5,095	5,947	85.7	16,323	18,164	89.9

[1] A full-time worker is a person who worked, mostly full-time, 50-52 weeks in 1971 and 49-52 weeks in 1982.

[2] Includes persons who have either completed or attended high school.

Source: Survey of Consumer Finances - 1972-1983, Unpublished Data. These data are herein published with the authorization of the Director, Household Survey Division.

$25,096 for males and $16,056 for females. And, as before, the gap for the ever-marrieds was an even bigger $10,056, or 39.4 percent, the divergence between $26,362 for men and $15,973 for women. Again, however, the never-married sample provides evidence that the true explanatory variable is not discrimination, but rather marital status. For in this case the difference between men at $18,164 and women at $16,323 was a very much smaller $1,841, equivalent to a gap of only 10.1 percent. (Undoubtedly much of this gap is explained by the well-known fact that women often choose careers in areas of employment which pay lower wages to both men and women.)

Such a conclusion can only be strengthened by a perusal of column 6, Table VII which describes the 1982 experience. Women's earnings as a percentage of men's does not fall below 80 percent for any of the never-married education categories, and rises above the 90 percent level for those with post secondary or university diplomas, the groups with the two highest educational attainments.

As well, the same trends were evident in 1971, as is seen by looking at both Tables VI and VII. The female-male earnings ratios at all educational levels was vastly higher for the never-marrieds than it was for the ever-marrieds. As shown by column 3, the female-male income ratio registers in the 70 percentile levels for the lower educational levels, and rises to the high 80s for post secondary schooling. Indeed, for never-marrieds with a post secondary degree, a female-male income ratio of 89.6 is virtually indistinguishable from exact equality. This is so when we remember that the data is adjusted for only education and marital status -- not age, experience, continuity in the labour force and career choice, to say nothing of statistically unverifiable phenomena such as perseverence, ambition, etc. Certainly this is compatible with the findings in this regard, of Professor Thomas Sowell mentioned above.

Women's earnings as a percentage of men's earnings in 1971 for never-marrieds with a university degree was 109.8 percent. This indicates that never-married women earned 9.8 percent *more* than their never-married male counterparts![46] Such a finding will appear to some people as an anomaly. This, at least, is the view of Statistics Canada. Certainly, it is difficult to reconcile this finding with a presumption of widespread discrimination against women. As well, it appears somewhat incompatible with statistics from other years (see Table VIII) which vary between 90.8 percent and 96.5 percent.

Table VIII

Year	"Single" Earners with university degree and working full-time		
	Average earnings ($)		
	Women	Men	Women's Earnings As % of Men's
1967	6,565	6,804	96.5
1973	10,418	11,475	90.8

Source: Letter to the Fraser Institute from R. Chawla, Senior Research Officer, Labour and Household Surveys Analysis Division, Statistics Canada, dated July 19, 1985.

However, this finding is so unexpected only because we have been led to believe that it is somehow "natural" for males to earn more than females, given employer discrimination against the latter. But there is nothing in economic theory which would lead to that result, and, as we have seen, the employer discrimination hypothesis itself has grave defects.

Discrimination

Another problem arises in the AR when it offers a definition of discrimination:

> Discrimination in this context means practices or attitudes that have, whether by design or impact, the effect of limiting an individual's or a group's right to the opportunities generally available because of attributed rather than actual characteristics. What is impeding the full development of the potential is not the individual's capacity but an external barrier that artificially inhibits growth. (p. 2)

At first glance, this would seem rather straight forward. As long as it is the actual, not attributed, characteristics that are relied upon in hiring (and these are relevant to the task at hand) no difficulty would arise. The trouble is, we live in a society of less than full information. Knowledge, rather than a given, is a scarce and precious resource.[47] In such a situation, while government bureaucrats may indeed have the funds at their disposal to conduct systematic research into "actual characteristics," their counterparts in the private sector, the employers, certainly do not. Instead, they are ofttimes perforce limited to relying on attributed characteristics as proxies for the underlying actual realities. When they act correctly (the attributed characteristics are good indications of the actual ones) no harm is done; actually, gains are made, since the actual characteristics are utilized in employment decisions in a cheap and efficient manner. But when errors are made (attributed characteristics are not unbiased estimators of actual ones) costs ensue. The employer chooses workers of lower productivity, and the more highly skilled are forced to fill job slots which less fully utilize their capacities. All that can be said for the market system, under such an assumption, is that at least it functions so as to reduce the error. Mistakes tend to be eliminated because those who make them, and hire unsuitable employees, earn lower profits than those who do not err, or who do so to a lesser degree. In contrast, when errors in hiring are made by Crown corporations,[48] there is no similar weeding out process, despite the resultant loss in productivity.

Systemic discrimination

The controversy over attributed versus actual characteristics also underlies the debate over systemic discrimination. The AR expresses itself on this phenomenon as follows:

> Rather than approaching discrimination from the perspective of the single perpetrator and the single victim, the systemic approach acknowledges that by and large the systems and practices we customarily and often unwittingly adopt may have an unjustifiably negative effect on certain groups in society. The effect of the system on the individual or group, rather than its attitudinal sources, governs whether or not a remedy is justified.
> Remedial measures of a systemic and systematic kind are the object of employment equity and affirmative action. They are meant to improve the situation for individuals who, by virtue of belonging to and being identified with a particular group, find themselves unfairly and adversely affected by certain systems or practices.

Systemic remedies are a response to patterns of discrimination that have two basic antecedents:

a) a disparately negative impact that flows from the structure of systems designed for a homogeneous constituency; and

b) a disparately negative impact that flows from practices based on stereotypical characteristics ascribed to an individual because of the characteristics ascribed to the group of which he or she is a member.

The former usually results in systems primarily designed for white able-bodied males; the latter usually results in practices based on white able-bodied males' perceptions of everyone else.

In both cases, the institutionalized systems and practices result in arbitrary and extensive exclusions for persons who, by reason of their group affiliation, are systematically denied a full opportunity to demonstrate their individual abilities. (pp. 9, 10)

Concern was expressed that certain job requirements demand irrelevant qualifications which have the effect of excluding disabled people from employment opportunity. The problem of irrelevant job requirements affects all four designated groups. Job requirements that have a disparate impact on certain groups need to be analyzed to determine whether or not they are justified. (p. 41)

But there are several fallacies in this way of looking at matters. Firstly, it is simply untrue that all discriminatory practices are based on "white able-bodied males' perceptions of everyone else." Yes, white able-bodied males do discriminate -- but they hardly have a monopoly over this practice. To mention just one other group, unmarried people of both genders who are looking to change that marital status also discriminate -- in favour of jobs which put them in contact with numerous eligible marriage partners. They may even be willing to accept pay cuts (what the economist calls "compensating differentials")[49] in order to compete for such jobs. For example, looking at the situation from the vantage point of males, a position which features an "advantageous" (low) male-female ratio of fellow workers, customers, etc., will tend to pay less, other things equal, than one in which the job holder will be in the proximity of large numbers of other men, and few eligible women. One thinks of the traditional logging or mining camp or the position of clerk in a store which sells men's shoes.[50]

The evidence

Secondly, the claim of "extensive exclusions" of people in groups who are discriminated against is incompatible with available evidence. One interpretation of an "exclusion" would be exclusion from the labour market itself. But as we have seen, from data collected by the AR, the labour force participation rates of women have been rising, and sharply so, in the last two decades. They rose in Canada from 30.1 percent in 1960 to 51.6 percent in 1982 (see p. 61, AR).

Nor can this contention be supported by the evidence on unemployment. Again, as shown by statistics compiled by the AR itself, while women have had slightly higher unemployment rates than men over the last two decades,[51] the differences have been small, hardly supportive of the charge of "extensive exclusion." In any case, in 1982, the last year for which such comparable data were available, the unemployment rate for males, 11.1 percent, was higher than that for females, which was 10.8 percent (see p. 78, AR).

Thirdly, the analysis of systemic discrimination is based on an implicit premise -- that labour force information is given to all, or costless (i.e., the assumption of perfect competition) -- which happens to be false.

Consider the following, a classical statement of this underlying premise:

> The conceptual experiment which measures discrimination is to change the race (religion, sex, etc.) of the individual and observe what happens to his economic position. A possible practical experiment would be to present employers with a set of job applications from workers that differ

solely in, say, their race and find out who would be hired. Discrimination could be inferred from a deviation in the selection process from that predicted by random sampling.[52]

Says Walter Williams of this view:

> Such an experiment is <u>not</u> a reliable measure of the existence or absence of racial tastes that may influence minority employment. The reason is that while the <u>experimenter</u> may have reliable information on the productivity of a particular employee, there is no reason at all to believe that the employer is similarly blessed. Even if the applicants have identical credentials by race, there is no reason why employers will <u>perceive</u> these credentials as equally creditable.[53]

Proxy variable

The point is that in a world of incomplete and costly information, race, or sex, or nationality, may be used as a proxy variable to predict the likelihood of successful employment; i.e., to find a productive employee. If, for example, women are more likely than men to leave the job for pregnancy and child care, or to have lower quality university degrees, or to be less highly motivated on the job and less attached to the labour force, then gender, which is inexpensive to utilize as a predictor of productivity, may be taken into account in order to minimize costs.

But suppose that gender turns out to be a poor prognosticator of high job productivity? If so, the marketplace itself will tend to correct the situation. Let us take a simplified numerical example to illustrate this process. Suppose that other things being equal (such as age, experience, credentials, etc.) businesspersons regard women as 70 percent as productive as men, while in actuality, they are really 110 percent as productive. If employers err in this manner, there is a profit opportunity open to the insightful entrepreneur. He or she can earn additional revenues by hiring undervalued women and firing (or refusing to hire or reducing through attrition) overvalued men.

So the tendency is for proxy variables to be accurate predictors of productivity. This is the only state of affairs compatible with equilibrium.[54]

Imperfect information

But is it "fair" to use proxies such as race, sex, national origin, etc., especially since they may, at any given time, be inaccurate? However much sense this question makes from some higher or philosophical perspective, it is entirely naive from the economic point of view -- one which takes into account the scarcity and thus costliness of information. In such a world, some sort of proxy must be used. There may be better proxies than gender. Perhaps physical or mental or psychological tests, height, weight, age, recommendations, resumes, interviews, trial periods, lie detectors, could be used. These are all far more costly than using gender as a criterion. Only if their increase in accuracy, if any, more than offsets their additional expenses, will they be utilized.

But their use only postpones the difficulty. None of these criteria, either, is perfectly accurate. Were they to be used, discrimination would still take place, only on the basis of these more complex proxies. Moreover, it is just such criteria to which the AR objects, on the grounds of systemic discrimination.

And, it must be readily admitted, tests, trial periods, strength, etc., can be the basis for systemic discrimination. Obviously, the market process of groping toward more and more accuracy will not satisfy Judge Abella. True to her concern with radical restructuring of society, she calls for no less than the elimination of proxies as a predictor of productivity. In a world of perfect information, such a policy would not be needed. In the present one, it would lead to a great loss in productivity if complied with.

Systemic discrimination and the AR

As we have seen, the concept of "systemic discrimination" is subject to serious reservations. Nevertheless, it will be of interest to explore how well the AR itself fares against the criticism that it is guilty of indulging in systemic discrimination.

How can we test such a hypothesis?

There are several possibilities. In order to do its work, the Abella Royal Commission contracted for 39 research papers relevant to its Terms of Reference. Brief descriptions of these, along with the names of the authors, are given in Appendix E (pp. 363-368). Of the 40 authors[55] for whom it was possible to determine gender, 27 were female, and 13 were male. As such, without any quota, or criterion of systemic discrimination, these are valueless statistics. So what benchmark shall we apply? If we use 50 percent - 50 percent as the measure of employment equality, then the Abella Royal Commission is clearly guilty of systemic discrimination against males, since it contracted for papers with more than twice as many females as males. But 50 percent isn't the only plausible cut-off point. Presumably, the prerequisite for even being considered as an author of an AR research document was being an economist. As noted above, only 28.4 percent of first professional degrees in economics in 1982 were attained by females.[56] Using this as the quota benchmark[57] the AR might be seen to be even more guilty of systemic discrimination, since they commissioned slightly over two-thirds of their research to women, who make up less than 30 percent of Canadian economists.

The staff

The second possibility is to enquire as to the makeup of the Abella Royal Commission personnel (see Appendix F, p. 370). Of the 35 employees, including Judge Rosalie Silberman Abella herself, fully 30 were female. Only 5 were male. This works out to 14.3 percent male and 85.7 percent female representation. If anything, then, the employment choices of the AR are even more indicative of systemic discrimination than is the pattern of its research contracts.

But there is a third possibility. The AR also consulted with no less than 154 professional economists in its deliberations (see Appendix C, pp. 330-336). And here it is bang-on, hitting the "perfect" 50 percent - 50 percent mark: Of the 154 consultants, 77 were male and 77 were female.

However, given that there are far more male than female economists in Canada, there may be reservations about the AR policy even if it did hit this target of exact equality, right on the button. Can we not say, with the Abella Report, that "motivations" are irrelevant; that "results" are all; that even in this case, the seeming equality is only an "effective signal" that discrimination has taken place? If so, then, the employment practices of the AR call for "remedial attention."

Rating the AR

So how does the AR rate as a discriminatory employer? Based on a superficial numerical analysis, it would presumably have to be judged as a discriminator regarding its contracted research papers and staff, and as a non-discriminator in its choices of consultants. But even this is by no means certain.

The point is that all such judgements are essentially arbitrary and subjective. Is the benchmark against which the AR hiring policy is to be judged all economists in the world, or just the ones in Canada? Is it to be the relevant subsection of the profession -- labour economists -- or is it to be a small part of this group -- those who have specialized in discrimination? Or is it to be an even smaller group, those who have intensively studied the so-called male-female earnings gap? There is, of course, no right answer. We can pick and choose as we wish. If we desire to see the AR as violating their own exhortations to "employment equality," there are a plethora of criteria upon which such a judgement could be based. Alternatively, were we to try to defend it against these charges, this might be more difficult, especially for their staff and research contracts, but it could be done.

No matter how you slice it, though, the AR is proposing a mandatory "employment equality" policy, using a standard upon which the AR itself could easily be judged to be in violation.

Profits and the discrimination hypothesis

We conclude this chapter on the economics of discrimination by considering one last weakness in the argument that equal pay legislation is justified because employer discrimination reduces female pay. In order to make this point, we must take a brief excursion into the economics of profit and equilibrium.

It is a popular misconception, perhaps understandable, that greater profits can be earned by firms which produce luxurious goods, than by those which create more plebian items. For example, it is commonly supposed that larger profits are recorded by Jaguar Motors than by Volkswagon;

that the incomes of real estate operators who located in high rent districts are in excess of those garnered in the slums.

Nothing, however, could be further from the truth. Were there any such incipient tendency in the marketplace, it would soon be corrected through the competitive struggle. For each company is a profit maximizer. Let returns be higher in one area of endeavour than another, and all would tend to flock from the latter to the former, pushing up profit rates where entrepreneurs were leaving, and reducing them in industries they were entering. That profits tend to be equated across all industries characterized by free entry and exit is thus one of the most basic axioms in all of economics.

What has all this to do with discrimination? Simple. There is an implication of the case in behalf of equal pay legislation that is impossible to reconcile with this economic postulate concerning profit. According to equal pay adherents such as the AR, employers exploit women. Through discrimination, they pay them less than they would otherwise. But if this is so, then the firms which employ women ought to attain greater returns than the ones which employ men -- who they presumably do not exploit, at least not to the same degree.

However, as we have seen, this is an exceedingly unlikely occurrence. For if the word ever got out that the female-dominated firms were more profitable than those which employ mostly males, investment would tend to shift from the latter to the former, once again equating profits. This process would also tend to bid up the wages of women and reduce those of men, as the former would now be in greater demand than the latter.

It is extremely difficult, unfortunately, to subject this economic analysis to empirical testing. Ideally, we would want to hold constant risk, capitalization, etc., across firms, while varying the proportion of male and female employees, and then measure any correlation between profit and gender. Our expectation is that profit rates would be independent of the sex of the workers. That is, that profit rates will not be positively correlated with the number, or percentage of females in the firm's labour force. The problem is that profit, risk and capitalization are all notoriously difficult to work with. These phenomena lack objective dimensions, and different accounting conventions provide a welter of complexity. In addition, while males and females are differentially represented among the professions, this does not hold for individual business concerns. Further, many females have jobs in the service, government, or voluntary sectors, in which profits are commonly not earned. All such employees would thus have to be disregarded for the purpose of our empirical examination -- and their elimination may bias any resultant findings.

Nevertheless, it is important that such work be attempted. It is highly unfortunate that the AR shows no evidence of even being aware of this problem.

CHAPTER 5

JOBS AND UNEMPLOYMENT

Yesterday's skills

The AR begins its analysis of education and training with what would appear to be virtually a truism:

> Jobs can realistically be made available only to those who are qualified to undertake them. No strategy designed to increase the participation of particular groups or individuals in employment systems can work unless the proposed employees have the skills to do the job. (p. 129)

> Although gaining these skills through education and training does not itself guarantee access to the labour force, it helps ensure that where there are jobs, a matching supply of qualified or qualifiable candidates is available. (p. 130)

The sentiments are widely shared. They find expression in such aphorisms as "you can't get today's jobs with yesterday's skills."

But the economist is highly suspicious of any statement which ignores prices, or, in this case, wages. The rejoinder, continually at the tip of his (or her) tongue is, "at what wage rate?" A person most certainly _can_ get today's jobs with yesterday's skills, or with virtually no skills at all, if the wage at which they offer themselves is at a low enough level. When this facet is incorporated into the analysis, the discussion turns to the appropriateness of the reduced wage at which low skilled people would find employment. But note, it is no longer a question of <u>whether</u> or not jobs would be available; they would be. We are only now concerned to point out that poorly skilled people will be poorly remunerated, in the marketplace.

Thus, the option open to the person with few job skills is not only to upgrade them and get a (relatively well-paid) job, but also to refrain from such investment in human capital, and attain more modestly paid employment. Consider the person who inhabits a poverty striken Third World country. Need he upgrade his skills to the level which would attract an offer of employment in an economically developed nation such as Canada? Of course not. Rather, he has the option, in the absence of laws which prohibit this, of attracting a job offer based on his present level of human capital.

Minimum wage legislation

However, it is a rather large leap of faith to assume that there will be no laws prohibiting an unskilled worker from attaining employment at wages commensurate with his abilities. In point of fact, there are numerous enactments which interfere in this regard. One in particular is called the minimum wage law. The AR has this to say in support of such legislation in its list of recommendations:

> 114. Sheltered workshops should pay disabled persons at least the <u>minimum wage.</u> They should also provide job placement services so that a greater number of disabled persons trained at these facilities are assisted in entering the workforce. Guidelines should be developed as to the duration, quality, and evaluation of training in sheltered workshop programs. (emphasis added) (p. 269)

Again, the AR finds itself in conformity with widespread public opinion on the matter, but again it is mistaken.

Widely trumpeted as the solution to the problem of low pay, public criticism has been limited to carping that the minimum wage level is not rising fast enough. This is particularly unfortunate since the long-run effect of the minimum wage law is, paradoxically, not to raise the take-home pay of workers with lesser skills, but often to make it well nigh impossible for them to find any jobs at all!

The major impetus behind this legislation is the fear that in its absence, employers would be completely free to dictate the level of wages paid. In this view, it would be a calamity for governments to leave remuneration decisions for the lowest paid workers to the "tender mercies" of the capitalist class. An entirely understandable stance. And, the argument that economists and the more enlightened minority spokespersons make against minimum wage laws does not deny that employers will try to pay as little as possible. On the contrary, those like ourselves who argue against minimum wage legislation fully accept the self-serving attitude of employers. But, we also recognize as an accurate description the harsh reality that there is an inexorable tendency for wage levels to reflect the productivity of workers. Wage levels below worker productivity are pushed up, those above pushed down, by the very actions of the self-serving employers.

Let us take for example a labourer who creates value of $5.00 per hour by dint of his efforts, and who is now being paid only $3.75 per hour. This means that the employer fortunate enough to have this labourer on his staff takes in $5.00 revenue for every hour of employment. Having to pay only $3.75, he makes a pure profit of $1.25 for each hour of employee toil. This sounds bad for the worker, but it is a highly unstable situation.

Unstable conditions

It cannot last because the $1.25 profit per employed hour acts like a vacuum to suck in competing uses of such profitable labour. Every other employer (potential and actual) would like nothing better than to woo this worker away from his present boss, employ him in his own firm, and seize these extraordinary profits for himself. Any would-be new employer, of course, can only entice the downtrodden worker with a better wage. An offer of $4.25 might do the trick and this would still leave a pure profit of 75¢ per hour. But this profit will continue to attract employers.

Where will this process end? As can be plainly seen, the upward march of wages toward $5.00 per hour will only cease when the profits to be gained by attracting a worker begin to fall below the information, transactions, and other costs of seeking him out and employing him. So we must conclude that in the absence of government intervention, a worker worth $5.00 per hour will tend to earn about $5.00 per hour.

But what happens with the passage of a law which says that if a firm hires this worker, it must pay $5.50 per hour? He will be forced into a life of unemployment! From the point of view of the prospective employer, taking on this labourer would be a financial disaster: $5.50 per hour will have to be paid out while only $5.00 per hour can be taken in. It may yet decide to act so unwisely in one or even a few cases, perhaps out of charity; but if the firm persists in such a policy on a large scale, it will only succeed in driving itself toward bankruptcy.

A mental experiment

Those still unconvinced of the power of a minimum wage law to price labour out of the market can try the following mental experiment. Trace the effects of a $25 per hour minimum wage law on workers with a $15 per hour productivity. It is easy to see that even such highly productive employees will be dismissed and replaced by fewer but still more highly skilled people, coupled with an influx of new, automated and highly sophisticated machinery.

The tragedy and the shame of this is that productivity levels of the low wage sector of the labour force, particularly the young, are usually raised by <u>working</u>: by showing up on time, by learning basic on-the-job skills, by becoming a reliable employee. If the low-productivity worker is but given a chance of employment, he can usually raise his skill levels above those rates now called for by law. With minimum wage legislation, however, these people are effectively barred from employment in the first place -- and the increased productivity that only on-the-job training can bring about. Instead, they are consigned to a life of enforced idleness, which brings in its wake many other problems.

Who are these people with low economic productivity who are so mistreated by this unwise public policy? They are largely to be found among teenagers, school dropouts, native and other rural peoples, immigrants who speak neither English nor French, alcoholics, and the handicapped. When two or more of these categories are combined, unemployment rates rise to astounding and astronomical levels. The most recent unemployment statistics for native peoples in B.C., for example, show rates for ill-educated, rural teenagers which reach as high as 50 percent -- and even these may be underestimates of the true problem -- as they ignore those who have left the labour force in despair.[58]

Raising pay scales?

We cannot leave this subject without asking why, if the minimum wage law is such a mistake, do the federal government and provinces continue to support this policy? The first reason is the electorates' well meaning fear of the exploitative employers mentioned above. This fear is one of the elements played on by the union movement -- the major institutional reason for the continuation of minimum wages.

The key point here is that unionized labour is always and ever in competition with non-organized and usually lower-productivity workers. Every time unions increase their own wage demands, employers are to that degree more tempted to substitute non-union labour. What better way to preclude this possibility than by lobbying for a minimum wage law which substantially increases the price of these alternative workers? By this process, unemployment which would otherwise be experienced by union members is visited upon those not permitted to offer themselves at a low enough wage.

Naturally, union spokespersons hide behind the cloak of "trying to raise wage levels for those at the bottom of the pay scale." But if this were _really_ their position, they could have no objection to a minimum wage law which applied only to unions, one that would prohibit unionists alone from earning any less, say, than $100 per hour. No responsible union leader could accept this challenge, because they would realize that the consequence would be massive unemployment for their members and a new, less remunerative career for themselves.[59]

CHAPTER 6

EQUAL PAY LEGISLATION

Barriers to entry

Equal pay legislation is another barrier which prevents, or impedes, the free flow of workers into job positions. Like minimum wages, these programs concentrate most of their ill effects on people at the bottom of the market skills and employment pyramid -- such as women, native peoples, minorities, the handicapped -- the very groups whose protection presumably serves as the focal point of the AR.

However, just as in the case of minimum wages, the AR, paradoxically, defends the very system most likely to be inimical to the welfare of its "client" groups. Says Judge Abella:

> Equal pay is an integral element in the implementation of employment equity. It must be included in any undertaking by employers to make the practices in the workplace more equitable.
> The existence of a gap between the earnings of men and women is one of the few facts not in dispute in the 'equality' debate. There are certainly open questions about it, the two main ones being the width of the gap and the right way to go about closing it. <u>But no one seriously challenges the reality that women are paid less than men, sometimes for the same work, sometimes for comparable work.</u> (emphasis added) (p. 232)

First of all, let it be said, once and for all, loud and clear, that the underlined statement is seriously mistaken. Contrary to this allegation, there are numerous "serious challenges" to this "reality." Five of them appear in the AR bibliography itself: four citations of Thomas Sowell (p. 390) and one of the present authors (p. 372).[60]
As well, states Morley Gunderson:

> On average, in Ontario and the rest of Canada, the female/male earnings ratio for full-time, full-year workers, <u>unadjusted</u> for differences in productivity related factors, is approximately .60. Adjustments for various productivity related factors such as experience, time worked, education, training, location, and occupation and industry tend to raise the adjusted ratio to approximately .75 - .85. Differences in experience and occupational distribution tend to be the most important determinants of the earnings differential. When productivity adjusted comparisons are made within the same narrowly-defined occupations within the same establishment -- the wage gap that is most relevant for equal pay legislation -- the adjusted ratio tends to be in the range of .90 - .95.[61]

Given the well-known impreciseness of the data, a female-male earnings ratio of .90 - .95, uncorrected for marital status, and socialization, and other hard-to-quantify variables, is tantamount to a finding that men and women are paid equally.

Equal pay

There are two main types of equal pay legislation: equal pay for equal work (EPFEW) and equal pay for work of equal value (EPFWOEV).

According to the first concept, if a man and a woman are doing the same job,[62] it shall be illegal to pay them different salaries. Assuming that the woman is being paid less, this stricture could be satisfied by either raising the hourly earnings of the female, or lowering those of the male.

However, the latter option is almost always precluded by EPFEW legislation, which insists that the woman's wage be raised, not that the man's wage be reduced. The AR gives its whole-hearted support to this practice, approvingly citing the fifth paragraph of Section 11 of the Canadian Human Rights Act:

> An employer shall not reduce wages in order to eliminate a discriminatory practice described in this section. (p. 242)

But this artificial boost in the minimuim wage payable to women will, in some cases, be tantamount to pricing them out of the market. As in the case of the minimum wage law, we do no favour to women by legislatively increasing their salaries -- at the cost of losing them the jobs in the first place.

The South African case

As well, EPFEW enactments "protect male jobs from low-wage female competition."[63] We can better understand this proposition by considering the economics of the Republic of South Africa. There, the white-racist unions advocate EPFEW as a *better means* than job reservation laws of protecting their jobs against the competition of lower paid black workers.[64] This is a paradox. In South Africa, EPFEW is advocated as a means of protecting a favoured group (white unionists), while in Canada it is urged as a way of helping an unfavoured group (females). It is simply not within the realm of possibility that both of these contrary analyses can be accurate. Only one can be correct; the other must be incorrect.

We may reward the Canadian feminists with greater moral stature than the South African white racist unions; certainly they are more well intentioned. But when it comes to economic insight, the South Africans have it all over the Canadians. Basic supply and demand analysis shows that when wages are boosted by legislative fiat, unemployment for the group in question ensues (South African blacks, Canadian women), and additional jobs and increased wages are the result for those competing with them (South African whites, Canadian males).

In South Africa, both job reservation and EPFEW laws are a means of freezing blacks out of higher paying jobs. The job reservation legislation specifically mentions which races shall be allowed to take which jobs. As such it is explicit, and racist. Nowhere in EPFEW legislation is race, as such, mentioned. Therefore, the racism is only implicit. But it is no less virulent, more so, in the view of some. Which is a better (more efficient) means of restricting black entry is purely an empirical question. However, were black and white productivity levels roughly comparable, then EPFEW would be a poor means indeed of achieving this end. Then, only the explicitly racist job reservation laws would be viable.[65] This is because being forced to pay blacks the same as whites would no longer make the hiring of blacks an economically destructive thing to do. But as long as black productivity is significantly below that of whites (and female productivity below that of males), then EPFEW legislation is a disaster for the economically and socially downtrodden groups.

A common vision

Let there be no misunderstanding on this point, however. The present authors, like those of the AR, share the vision of both EPFEW and EPFWOEV. Indeed, in our view, the marketplace tends to bring about equal pay for equal productivity, no matter which of the two definitions of equality is employed. As we have seen, any deviation from this situation sets up market forces (see discussion of "redheads" above, pp. 6, 7) which tend to be corrective.

There is a difference between us and the AR, however, and it is a vast one. First of all, we favour the voluntary forces of the market, not the employment of coercive legislation. Just because a certain outcome is desired, this does not imply that legislative remedies are necessary or wise. For example, there is a tendency for profits to equalize over the various industries of a nation; this hardly justifies an "equal profits law," requiring that profits in each industry be equal to those earned everywhere else.

Secondly, and perhaps of far greater practical importance, the definition of equal productivity is far different in the actual marketplace than it is in the ivory towered halls of the legislature.

In the hurly-burly of the business world, the productivity which is equally remunerated is defined in terms of the profit statement. He or she who adds to the firm's revenues is rewarded proportionately. Those enterprises which either overpay or underpay tend to go bankrupt. The former case is obvious. If a firm overpays its employees, it loses out in the competitive struggle. But the latter case is no less true. If a company underpays (that is, pays below the marginal productivity of its workers) it will tend to lose its employees to competitors. It will suffer from over-optimal quit rates, and dissatisfied employees. It will thus have to invest in additional and costly hiring, firing and training expenses.

No accident

It is hardly an accident that there is a vital and healthy management consulting industry which specializes in giving employers advice about salary conditions in the marketplace. Basically, the ability to estimate the productivity of an employee is an entrepreneurial one. It calls for no mean level of talent and ability, and willingness to bear risk. It requires the assessment of such subjective and imponderable characteristics as ambition, intelligence, perserverance, initiative, knowledge, skill, ability to work as a team member (or not, as the case may be). Further, there is the problem, especially in small firms, that each prospective employee must be able to interact well with the boss. (This is a crucial dimension of productivity, and is entirely subjective.)

In stark contrast, the equal pay arising from such legislative initiatives has nothing whatever to do with productivity in the economic sense. Rather, it would be predicated upon highly imperfect proxy variables for productivity such as age, education, experience, hours of work and other similar quantifiable and objective criteria.[66] But these values at best are only remotely related to productivity, as outlined above.

It is one of the basic flaws of the entire AR that nowhere in it do we find even any mention, let alone analysis of, the concept of marginal revenue productivity (what we have been referring to as "economic productivity").

Intrinsic worth

Next, consider the following statement:

> Equality means nothing if it does not mean that we are of equal worth regardless of differences in gender, race, ethnicity, or disability. The projected, mythical, and attributed meaning of these differences cannot be permitted to exclude full participation. (p. 3)

In one possible interpretation, this makes perfect sense; that is, in terms of political equality. Certainly, there is no one in this country who would care to deny that all Canadians, regardless of differences in gender, race, ethnicity, or disability, have the right to vote, to equal justice under our laws, to the same consideration due all citizens, to equal treatment under our Charter of Rights and Freedoms.

The problem with the AR in this regard is that it is trying to transfer, from the political realm to the economic, what is an axiom in the former, but not the latter. Legislated equal worth is a basic tenet in the political sphere, but it is simply false, and even pernicious, in the economic.

Harsh though this may seem, we are not all of equal worth in the marketplace. Contrary to what occurs in politics, we have no intrinsic worth whatever in economics. It all depends on supply and demand.

In the case of EPFWOEV, third-party "experts" will be called upon to determine whether mainly male occupations, such as truck driver, are "really" of equal value to jobs held mostly by females, such as secretary. A spurious scientific objectivity will be imparted by numerically rating such aspects of these callings as training, responsibility, working conditions, education, etc., and then adding them together to derive a total point score. Say what you will about such a scheme, at least it has one undoubted advantage; it will serve as a full employment measure for lawyers; for the values assigned to each dimension can only be arbitrary. The procedure will thus open society up to a spate of contentious lawsuits, as the various newly created pressure groups endlessly strive for more favourable ratings.

Objective values?

The point is, there is no such thing as an intrinsic or objective "worth"[67] of a job, (nor of goods and services such as paper clips, music lessons, etc.). On the market, crucial in the evaluation of employment slots is the subjective rank-orderings of the consumers -- the willingness of people to pay for things. The job of whip-maker, horse-trainer or carriage-wright might have required tremendous investments in skill, and great responsibility. But with the invention of the horseless carriage, and in the face of fickle consumer preferences, all this goes for naught. Were there such, the expert job evaluators at the turn of the century might have given these tasks high point totals. But on the market, that is, in reality, these jobs were suddenly rendered obsolete and valueless.

Presently, the jobs of dentists, dental hygienists, teeth x-ray technicians, all require much intelligence, years of intensive training, great diagnostic skills and a high level of professionalism. Were the evaluators unleashed upon these jobs to work their magic, there is no doubt at all that a high point total would ensue. But if and when a cure for tooth decay is found, these skills will go the way of the dodo bird, as far as value is concerned. Consumers will no longer be willing to purchase their services, and the returns to human capital invested in these lines will fall precipitously.

Let us consider one more example. Suppose that female prison guards do exactly the same quality and kind of work as is done by male prison guards. We assume, in other words, that male and female prison guards do "equal work." But let us suppose that for some reason women are far more reluctant to enter this profession than are men.[68] Under such conditions, in the marketplace, female prison guards will receive higher salaries than their male colleagues. This, according to the logic of the EPFEW philosophy, is obviously "unfair."

Solutions

What can be done? If the female wage rate is lowered to that of the male, there will not be a great enough supply of women prison guards to satisfy the demand. If the male wage rate is increased to match that of the female, there will be an over supply of male prison guards. If the wage rate of both is set at some intermediate point, there will be an excess supply of men prison guards and a shortage of women prison guards.[69] If the expert evaluators take into account this phenomenon too in their evaluations of male and female prison guard jobs (as well as all other unquantifiable factors which determine wage rates), they will escape the quandary of creating either a shortage and/or surplus of prison guards, but two anomalies will obtain.

First, the results will be incompatible with equal pay notions of fairness. If the unequal reluctance of males and females to enter this profession is considered by the evaluators, they will have to award more points to the female guards. Since by stipulation they do the "same work," this would be "unfair."

Secondly, and more basically, if the evaluators take into account all phenomena that determine wages in the economy, of what possible use can they be? At best, they will no more than replicate the pattern of wages established on the marketplace. More likely, they will only imperfectly succeed in achieving this goal. After all, entrepreneurs succeed or fail in business to a great degree based on how closely they can tailor wage rates to productivity levels. The compensation of the "experts," in contrast, will depend more on how well they satisfy their political constituencies. If there is, at best, only imperfect success in duplicating the market pattern of wages, this process will misallocate labour throughout the economy.

It landed I know not where

Consider in this regard the following statement:

>...let us assume a skill which is objectively difficult and reflects much objectively measurable training on the part of its practitioner; but let us also suppose it is a skill no one is interested in. Consider a person who is adept at throwing arrows into the air and catching them with his teeth. This is extremely difficult to do, and takes endless practice. Basketball players earning six-figure salaries do nothing so demanding. Unhappily, nobody wants to hire our man to catch arrows. He must eke out a living as a street entertainer. Is he

somehow being denied his intrinsic worth by passers-by who flip him quarters? Does a circus scout who offers him a pittance for his act undershoot what the knack entitles him to? The answers would seem to be no. Intrinsic moral and aesthetic merit aside, the skill is economically worthless - unable to command other goods and services - if no one will pay for it. Only someone willing to trade something for the service in question can confer economic worth on it.[70]

Canada has only recently emerged from a bout of wage price controls. The Anti Inflation Board led to inefficiency, inflexibility and increased bureaucratization of the economy. EPFEW and EPFWOEV are merely different kinds of wage controls, masquerading under a cloud of moral platitudes. As wage controls, they will have detrimental effects on the economy, similar to those imposed by our experiment with AIB. The move toward EPFEW and EPFWOEV should be resisted on this ground alone.

CHAPTER 7

JOB TRAINING

Public sector job training programs

Let us now turn to the views of the AR on job training. To be sure, this is a crucial problem. For on the one hand, there were in the early 1980s some one million Canadians out of work, almost ten percent of the labour force. While on the other hand, there were at this time numerous jobs going begging -- in the high technology, engineering, computer science, electrician, machinist, tool and die-making fields, in the western provinces, the territories, and in outlying districts all over the country -- but the unemployed seemed not to have the requisite skills to fill these jobs.

Into this shambles, enter the AR with a flawed analysis of the problem, and a series of recommendations that would further entrench the role of the public sector, and reduce the freedom and initiative of the private sector.

And its recommendations? A vast overhaul of job training programs in this country to ensure a match between "training opportunities" and "job prospects." (p. 159) The "comprehensive plan" calls for more training allowances, additional training centres, increased emphasis on the needs of women, native persons, the handicapped and visible minorities, a move toward general (generic) and away from specific training, a rise in job forecasting efforts and greater publicity for the entire program. As well, employers are to be encouraged to take part.[71]

On its face, this sounds like a reasonable response to the problem. If job slots in some fields are going unfilled, in the face of hordes of potential employees with skills -- but of the wrong kinds -- then what could be more appropriate than a government plan to tailor training to job requirements?

Crystal-ball gazing

This sounds good, but it is actually wrongheaded, and counterproductive. For training takes <u>time</u>. Weeks and months for low levels of skill, years in order to learn the kinds of technology now needed by modern industry. And during the necessary retraining time, the requirements of industry have a nasty habit of changing. There is no guarantee, that is, that when the graduates of the overhauled job-training programs advocated by the AR are ready to re-enter the labour force, industry will still require the skills they have learned, whether general or specific. Forecasting future manufacturing needs, and matching these to training programs, is a task calling for the coordination of the marketplace. Only it can reward those with an ability to pick the winners -- and penalize those who cannot. There is no evidence that the Ministry of Labour has ever had this talent in the past, or any indication that it has learned how to accomplish this in the future.[72]

On the contrary, all evidence points to the opposite conclusion.

The present system, for which government bears ultimate responsibililty, has created numerous "horror stories": the Newfoundland technical college which has graduated students in electronics who were trained with obsolete tube-type equipment; a Montreal community college with no computer department, even though there were many such unfilled positions nearby; the Cape Breton fishing industry, which had to import technical assistance from Boston, because none of the local colleges offered courses in the repair and maintenance of newly installed electronic fish-finding equipment.[73]

Moreover, the Adult Occupational Training Act has been in effect for almost the last two decades. And yet, Canada is saddled with the very problem Judge Abella now seeks to correct. Why should this outmoded system of government job-training initiatives be given yet another chance, when it has failed so often, and so dismally, in the past? To expect the AR recommendations to succeed -- this time -- is like expecting the fox to do a better job of guarding the chicken coop than she did -- last time.

No, the real solution to this problem lies in other directions:

Unemployment insurance

Before anything at all can be done about unemployment, we must have a clear idea of how serious the problem really is. Present statistics hide almost more than they show, in part because of the liberal Unemployment Insurance program in Canada. This encourages people to declare themselves "unemployed" -- whether they really are or not -- in order to collect the benefits. It over-stimulates seasonal work, where it is easier to attain "unemployed" status. According to Fraser Institute calculations,[74] this one program alone is responsible for boosting registered unemployment rates by about 2.3 percentage points in 1985. This sounds almost insignificant, but actually represents 21 percent of the unemployment rate. In other words, one in five of the unemployed is induced into that position by the availability of unemployment compensation at the generous levels provided in Canada.

It is a matter for reflection, even if precise comparisons are difficult, that at the moment U.S. unemployment rates are some four percentage points lower than those in Canada, while U.I. benefits in the U.S. are 0.8 percent of G.N.P. and 2.3 percent of Canadian G.N.P.

Labour mobility

If we want to match jobs and people, we must realize that new employment opportunities are likely to pop up anywhere at all. In a resource-based economy, new jobs tend to follow the path of new discoveries -- and these are no respecters of present settlement patterns in Canada.

This means that labour mobility must be as smooth and easy as possible. Yet, in the event, provincial and local governments have placed barriers on interprovincial labour (and job-creating capital) mobility. Mayor Ralph Klein's bigoted outburst about putting job-seeking "bums" from eastern Canada in Calgary's jails is only the latest entry in a rather unfortunate chapter of our economic history. B.C. Premier Bill Bennett implied virtually the same thing when he scotched an attempt by Canadian Pacific to invest in forestry giant McMillan-Bloedel by saying that "B.C. is not for sale."

And numerous provinces, from one end of the country to the other, give preferential treatment to indigenous capital and labour -- another form of discrimination against labour and labour mobility.[75]

Job training

The difficulty facing Canadian job training programs is how to pick the winners: the skills that will be needed, starting in the next few months and years, and continuing, if possible, for the next two or three decades as well.

There are, ultimately, two means to this end. Under the present system, society puts its eggs all in one basket. Money is channelled from numerous sources in the private sector toward a single training "czar," as urged by Judge Abella, in this case. We hope and pray that the bureaucrats in charge will choose wisely, for a large part of the future of the entire economy is in their hands.

The other system, oddly enough, is called free enterprise. Here, the relevant tax monies remain in private hands, and individuals, firms and corporations are free to enter the training industry. In the natural course of events, some will be winners, able to peer into the future, and prepare their students accordingly, and others will not. This will be beneficial, for with numerous competitors, many options will be tried. The failures will learn from the successes, first in order to earn greater profits and secondly, in order to stave off bankruptcy.

This idea may sound novel to sophisticated people living in a mixed economy in the latter part of the 20th century, and used to a virtual government monopoly of training efforts. But this system, free enterprise, is the one largely responsible for the marvellous standard of living enjoyed in the western democracies. It can work, and work well, in the task of job training, if only we allow it. The task of converting a centralized-statist job training and education system into a decentralized private industry is indeed a great challenge. But it is well worth undertaking, and must be implemented, if our training crisis is to be solved.[76]

Privatization

We must conclude that there is little need for an upgraded public sector role for matching people with jobs; on the contrary, government has been tried, and found wanting. Government bureaucrats have in the past guessed incorrectly,[77] all too often, about the future path of the Canadian economy, and the job skills which would later be required. That is why we are now in the present mess. Who is Judge Abella to now presume she can pick the winners, the national occupations of the next decades? Far better to leave this responsibility to numerous entrepreneurs who themselves bear the risks of failure.

It is of great importance that the politicians and bureaucrats put their own house in order: one, by ending the barriers to interprovincial mobility they themselves have erected, and two, by leaving the labour retraining business to the private sector.

CHAPTER 8

CONCLUSION

Egalitarian philosophy

Our main criticism of the AR is not the egalitarian philosophy which permeates it but rather the unsatisfactory economic analysis employed by it. The main methodological fault of the AR is that it makes no effort to explore any alternative to the "employer discrimination is responsible for the female-male wage gap" hypothesis. Instead, it simplistically assumes that since this gap exists (a point very much open to question, as we have seen) the employer must be responsible.

From this base, it goes on to argue for affirmative action -- but without taking any cognizance of the harm done to disadvantaged groups by this policy. Worse, it attempts to evade these problems by semantic means: substituting the new phrase "employment equity" for the discredited "quotas," "affirmative action," and "reverse discrimination," even though the former is no more than a synonym for the latter.

Another shortcoming is that although the AR cites several relevant Fraser Institute studies in its reference material, it shows no evidence of even considering one of its most important findings: that marital status, and the unequal family, home, and child care responsibilities it engenders, is a crucial element in understanding the female-male income gap.

Invalid argument

Although the AR combines an unsatisfactory economic analysis with a strong egalitarian philosophy, this is by no means a necessary connection. Indeed, it is possible to combine a strong adherence toward gender equality with an economic perspective which analyzes the female-male earnings gap in terms of early child socialization and marital and family relations, not employer discrimination; and, moreover, which contains an accurate assessment of the negative impact of affirmative action programs.

Such an accomplishment has been attained by Conrad Winn, who states:

> The point of departure for this essay is that society ought to equalize income between genders. However, the empirical evidence shows that affirmative action in the federal government, particularly quota hiring, is based on a false picture of the causes of the gender income gap and on an incomplete picture of the consequences of affirmative action. The gender gap is not caused primarily by employer discrimination but by educational segregation and by heavy and unequal family burdens.
> The proponents of quota hiring for women overlook the unintended societal impacts of the program. In the name of equality and justice, affirmative action does injustice to low-income women, to low-status men, and to mothers who work at home.[78]

Winn, too, cites the Fraser Institute book <u>Discrimination, Affirmative Action, and Equal Opportunity</u>.[79] But instead of merely listing it in his references, he shows evidence of having come to grips with its findings. One example has to do with the importance of such unquantifiable variables as culture and personal motivation.[80] On the gender gap, states Winn,

> One view holds that there is no gender gap, that income differences are fully explained by differences in qualifications and willingness to work. This view is given plausibility by evidence showing that single women earn as much or more than single men with the same qualifications and that women who are willing to relocate do as well as men who are willing to relocate.[81]

And again,

> The view that there is really no gender gap is buttressed by the evidence that married women in the workforce, especially those with children at home, are less interested in full-time work, have less time available for work, engage in less promotion-seeking behaviour, and express less interest in promotion when asked.[82]

Earnings

With regard to marital status and income, Winn finds that:

> The very substantial responsibilities of child-rearing and their unequal distribution explain why single women achieve more occupational success than married women.[83]

And on the career consequences of parenthood, Winn cites Fraser authors Hoffman and Reed at length:

> In general, the effects of parenthood were like those of marriage, only more so. It increased men's desires for promotion and their efforts to achieve it, and decreased both among women. The male and female clerks in our sample did not differ in their desire for additional children; 43% of the women and 42% of the men intended to have them. But the effects would be quite different: 17% of the women who planned to have children did not intend to remain in the labour force until retirement; only 4% of the men who planned to have children expressed an intention to leave, a figure virtually identical to those for male and female clerks who did not plan to have more children. Similarly, 28% of the female clerks who had children had been out of the labour force in the past compared to 3% of the fathers in our sample...(C)hildless female clerks, and male clerks whether they had children or not, were likely to have worked overtime and to report that they were

available for any shift assignment, while mothers of children under eighteen, not surprisingly, reported less flexibility.[84]

Winn concludes from this analysis that:

> The empirical evidence of the special responsibility for child-rearing shouldered by women corresponds closely to public perceptions of the nature of family life and the work world.[85]

It is unfortunate for AR, which shares Winn's objectives, that it did not more carefully, and critically, examine the evidence available to it. In large measure, misdiagnosis of the problem -- or perhaps an unwillingness to accept the implications of obvious symptoms -- have produced suggested cures which will not only be ineffective but actually harmful.

Postscript

In the United States, the legislated equal pay "movement" has, if not been dealt a death blow, at least been halted dead in its tracks. According to the Equal Employment Opportunity Commission, in a unanimous ruling, the law of the land does not necessitate employers to pay equal wages for jobs which on some artificially constructed scale have comparable worth.[86]

Says Clarence Thomas, the chairman of the five-member Federal Commission:

> Sole reliance on a comparison of the intrinsic value of dissimilar jobs which command different wages in the market does not prove a violation of Federal law. We are convinced that Congress never authorized the Government to take on wholesale restructuring of wages that were set by non-sex-based decisions of employers, by collective bargaining or by the marketplace.[87]

In Canada, by contrast, the movement for equal pay legislation is alive and well, if not as vibrant as its advocates might wish it to be.

It was originally thought that any new legislation brought down by the Progressive Conservative government would be based on the recommendations of the AR, and would thus demand that private companies attempting to win federal contracts produce affirmative action plans as a precondition. However, this has been watered down somewhat. The legislation tabled in July 1985 requires only that firms seeking contracts worth $200,000 or more declare themselves to be "equal opportunity employers." According to the Globe and Mail, this

> will mean it could take up to four years for a company to be cut off from such contracts for failing to improve the job prospects of women and other disadvantaged workers.[88]

While this enactment thus falls short of the more extreme measures urged by the AR, it is a dangerous if somewhat more tentative foray into the dangerous thickets of legislated equal pay-ism. Based on the findings of the present study, appropriate public policy would call for a jettisoning of the entire idea -- the path on which the U.S. seems to be heading.

NOTES

1   It is doubtless true that quotas will ensure equal employment opportunities as well. For example, a law compelling all large companies to hire redheads in proportion to their percentage of the general population can be expected to accomplish this goal. But there are serious difficulties. First, as we have seen, a group must become politically powerful enough to ensure this (even homosexuals, with their heavy political clout, have not so far been able to enforce employment quotas on their own behalf). In contrast, in the marketplace, no political power at all is needed. Secondly, quotas have strong negative unintended consequences for those minority groups who are "protected" by them. (See literature cited in Note 9, below.) Thirdly, affirmative action programs are very costly. Estimates for the U.S. in fiscal 1976 came to $329,296,367. This congressional research figure includes the costs of the federal government alone -- completely ignoring other government levels and impacts on the private sector. (See John H. Bunzel, "Affirmative Action, Negative Results," Hoover Institute Reprint #30, originally in Encounter, November 1979.)

2   It is important to realize that this painstaking, step-by-step bidding process up from $300 is only a mental experiment to show the underlying economic principles. In the real world, were prejudice against redheads to manifest itself, their wages would in all probability rise quickly to the $400 level or, even more likely, not fall much below $400 in the first place.

3   James Buchanan and Gordon Tullock, The Calculus of Consent: The Logical Foundation of Constitutional Democracy (Ann Arbor: University of Michigan Press, 1971); Ludwig von Mises, The Clash of Group Interests and Other Essays, New York: Center for Libertarian Studies, 1978; Murray N. Rothbard, For a New Liberty, New York: Collier-Macmillan, 1978, pp. 206-207.

4   Constance Baker Motley, "The Legal Status of the Black American," in The Black American Reference Book, ed.

Mabel M. Smythe (Englewood Cliffs, New Jersey: Prentice-Hall, 1976), pp. 101-102; Jack Greenberg, Race Relations and American Law (New York: Columbia University Press. 1959), pp. 80-86 and Appendix, p. 372. See also Act of the General Assembly of the State of Louisiana Providing for Separate Railway Carriages for the White and Colored Races #111, 1890, p. 152; and Plessey v. Ferguson, 163 U.S. 537 (1896), wherein the U.S. Supreme Court upheld this State of Louisiana legislative enactment.

5   See, for example, Motor Carrier Act of British Columbia, 1960, Chapter 252, consolidated on September 21, 1978, sections 5-17; Louisiana, Public Utilities Revised Statute 33: 4403, 4404, 1948: South Carolina, Motor Vehicle Carriers, 1940, Chapter 23, article 15; New York State Transportation Corporations Law, 1926, Chapter 63, article 5. See also "Negro Group Is Ordered to Halt Bus Service Here," New York Times, January 3, 1968, p. 36; "Negro Group Seeks to Buy City Buses," New York Times, January 4, 1968, p. 27, which describes the plight of the National Economic Growth and Reconstruction Organization (N.E.G.R.O.), which was ordered to stop operating an unfranchised bus service in Queens, New York; "Negro Bus Line Enjoined," New York Times, January 5, 1968, p. 32; "Where Blacks Own the Bus," Business Week, May 15, 1971, p. 78.

6   Armen A. Alchian and Reuben A. Kessel, "Competition, Monopoly and the Pursuit of Money," in Aspects of Labour Economics, National Bureau of Economic Research, Princeton: Princeton University Press, 1962.

7   A competitive industry is defined not in terms of concentration, but on the basis of rivalry and free entry. See Donald Armstrong, Competition Versus Monopoly, Vancouver: The Fraser Institute, 1982; and Walter Block, A Response to the Framework Document for Amending the Combines Investigation Act, Vancouver: The Fraser Institute, 1982.

8   Rosalie Silberman Abella, Equality in Employment: A Royal Commission Report, Ottawa, Ministry of Supply

and Services Canada, 1984. Unless otherwise specified, all unidentified quotes shall be from this Report.

9   Previous Fraser Institute research had focused on the fundamental difference between the public and private sectors; it showed that in the latter, but not the former case, the profit and loss system tends to retard discriminatory behaviour in the labour market. Even in the public sector (and certainly in the private), a female-male wage gap is by no means overwhelming evidence of employer discrimination. Other factors --type of education, labour force attachment, marital status, early childhood socialization, choice of occupation -- can, and do, explain the male-female wage differential. The Abella Report relies instead on those academics who choose to label as discrimination any male-female differentials which cannot be explained in terms of such variables as age, years of education, university credentials, unionization, etc. But this is illegitimate, since there is no evidence which independently shows that these statistical "residuals" are indeed due to discrimination. See in this regard, Discrimination, Affirmative Action, and Equal Opportunity, Walter Block and Michael A. Walker, eds., Vancouver: The Fraser Institute, 1982; Walter Block and Walter Williams, "Male-Female Earnings Differentials: A Critical Reappraisal," Journal of Labour Research, Vol. II, No. 2, Fall 1981, pp. 385-388; Walter Block, "Directions for Future Research in Equal Pay Legislation," Towards Equity: Proceedings of a Colloquium on the Economic Status of Women in the Labour Market, Muriel Armstrong, ed; Ottawa: The Economic Council, 1985, pp. 119-21, 134-35, 179-82.

10 It is true that these Terms of Reference also contain the phrase, "...analysis contained in reports... indicate the need for further government action to encourage, in all sectors of economic activity, the hiring, training and promotion of women, native people, disabled persons, and visible minorities"; (p. i). This does not deny, however, that the mandate given the Abella Report was limited to Crown and Government of Canada corporations.

11 AR, pp. 372, 390.

12 Robert Nozick defends the entitlement or process theory of justice in property titles, as against an end-state, condition, or principle of distribution theory. He argues that given a fair or proper initial endowment, any wealth distribution which results from a fair process (no force, no fraud, no theft, etc.) is just. States Nozick:

> It is not clear how those holding alternative conceptions of distributive justice can reject the entitlement conception of justice in holdings. For suppose a distribution favored by one of these non-entitlement conceptions is realized. Let us suppose it is your favorite one and let us call this distribution D_1; perhaps everyone has an equal share, perhaps shares vary in accordance with some dimension you treasure. Now suppose that Wilt Chamberlain is greatly in demand by basketball teams, being a great gate attraction. (Also suppose contracts run only for a year, with players being free agents.) He signs the following sort of contract with a team: In each home game, twenty-five cents from the price of each ticket of admission goes to him. (We ignore the question of whether he is "gouging" the owners, letting them look out for themselves.) The season starts, and people cheerfully attend his team's games; they buy their tickets, each time dropping a separate twenty-five cents of their admission price into a special box with Chamberlain's name on it. They are excited about seeing him play; it is worth the total admission price to them. Let us suppose that in one season one million persons attend his home games, and Wilt Chamberlain winds up with $250,000, a much larger sum than the average income and larger even than anyone else has. Is he entitled to this income? Is this new distribution D_2, unjust? If so, why? There is

no question about whether each of the people was entitled to the control over the resources they held in D_1; because that was the distribution (your favorite) that (for the purposes of argument) we assumed was acceptable. Each of these persons chose to give twenty-five cents of their money to Chamberlain. They could have spent it on going to the movies, or on candy bars, or on copies of Dissent magazine, or of Monthly Review. But they all, at least one million of them, converged on giving it to Wilt Chamberlain in exchange for watching him play basketball. If D_1 was a just distribution, and people voluntarily moved from it to D_2, transferring parts of their shares they were given under D_1 (what was it for if not to do something with?) isn't D_2 also just? If the people were entitled to dispose of the resources to which they were entitled (under D_1), didn't this include their being entitled to give it to, or exchange it with, Wilt Chamberlain? Can anyone else complain on grounds of justice? Each other person already has his legitimate share under D_1. Under D_1, there is nothing that anyone has that anyone else has a claim of justice against. After someone transfers something to Wilt Chamberlain, third parties still have their legitimate shares; their shares are not changed. By what process could such a transfer among two persons give rise to a legitimate claim of distributive justice on a portion of what was transferred, by a third party who had no claim of justice on any holding of the others before the transfer? To cut off objections irrelevant here, we might imagine the exchanges occurring in a socialist society, after hours. After playing whatever basketball he does in his daily work, or doing whatever other daily work he does, Wilt Chamberlain decides to put in overtime to earn additional money. (First his work quota is set; he works time over that.) Or imagine it is a skilled juggler people like to see, who puts on shows after hours.

Why might someone work overtime in a society in which it is assumed their needs are satisfied? Perhaps because they care about things other than needs. I like to write in books that I read, and to have easy access to books for browsing at odd hours. It would be very pleasant and convenient to have the resources of Widener Library in my back yard. No society, I assume, will provide such resources close to each person who would like them as part of his regular allotment (under D_1). Thus, persons either must do without some extra things that they want, or be allowed to do something extra to get some of these things. On what basis could the inequalities that would eventuate be forbidden?

Notice also that small factories would spring up in a socialist society, unless forbidden. I melt down some of my personal possessions (under D_1) and build a machine out of the material. I offer you, and others, a philosophy lecture once a week in exchange for your cranking the handle on my machine, whose products I exchange for yet other things, and so on. (The raw materials used by the machine are given to me by others who possess them under D_1, in exchange for hearing lectures.) Each person might participate to gain things over and above their allotment under D_1. Some persons even might want to leave their job in socialist industry and work full-time in this private sector. I shall say something more about these issues in the next chapter. Here I wish merely to note how private property even in means of production would occur in a socialist society that did not forbid people to use as they wished some of the resources they are given under the socialist distribution

D_1. The socialist society would have to forbid capitalist acts between consenting adults.

The general point illustrated by the Wilt Chamberlain example and the example of the entrepreneur in a socialist society is that no end-state principle or distributional patterned principle of justice can be continuously realized without continuous interference with people's lives. Any favored pattern would be transformed into one unfavored by the principle, by people choosing to act in various ways; for example, by people exchanging goods and services with other people, or giving things to other people, things the transferrers are entitled to under the favored distributional pattern. To maintain a pattern one must either continually interfere to stop people from transferring resources as they wish to, or continually (or periodically) interfere to take from some persons resources that others for some reason chose to transfer to them.

Anarchy, State and Utopia, New York: Basic Books, 1974, pp. 160-163.

13 The total cost of the Abella Report was in the neighbourhood of $1.1 million. (In contrast, expenditure on the average Fraser Institute volume of equal length is between $70,000 - $90,000.)

14 For example, enhanced wealth. If we eschewed these benefits which society makes possible, most people now living would die of starvation.

15 Nor could we even know them. Consider the example of the lowly pencil, offered by Milton Friedman, Free to Choose, New York: Harcourt Brace Jovanovich, 1980. The rubber, tin, lead, glue, paint may be manufactured by people living on 5 different continents, speaking literally dozens of languages. How many of us really

have the desire to have full access to such decision-making processes?" Most people are content to have limited access to such processes, limited, in most cases, to the choice of purchasing them or not.

16 Suppose there were a "machine" (see Robert Nozick, op. cit., pp. 42-45) which could homogenize the population in all these characteristics; that is, after being subjected to it, all Canadians would have equality in all these attributes (and whatever other ones were deamed by anyone to be "unfairly" spread around at present). Would it be "fair" to force all our citizens, kicking and screaming as they went, to enter into this machine? The result might be the egalitarian's idea of heaven, but to many this would be a stultifying and boring vision of hell, Brave New World style.

17 A particularly victimized group consists of bald middle aged males who are advocates of the free enterprise system. The stories we could relate on this unusually vicious and depraved sort of discrimination ....

18 This legislation has led to violent outbreaks. In Islamabad, Pakistan, for example, a student riot in protest of a rule reserving certain sections of buses for women resulted in death and injury. See the Vancouver Province, February 6, 1984.

19 See Thomas Sowell, Knowledge and Decisions, New York: Basic Books, 1980, pp. 252, 3.

20 This interpretation is only reinforced by the fact that the employer will be "advised" by the enforcement agency to amend these "practices," if the "results are found to be unreasonably low."

21 The present authors wish to express a debt of gratitude to Professor Walter Williams for making this point.
    Thomas Sowell has amassed numerous cases of such "under-representation," or inversely, "over-representation" of other minority groups. (If one race, sex or nationality is over-represented, then the others, on average, must be under-represented.) For example, Jews

are disproportionately urban, Germans are overrepresented in the beer industry, there are more Irish policemen in the U.S. than would be expected based on an analysis of their population size. See Sowell, Ethnic America, New York: Basic Books, 1981; idem., The Economics and Politics of Race, New York: William Morrow and Co., Inc., 1983.

22 The idea that employers of architects and engineers should be more discriminatory than employers of computer operators appears counter-intuitive. At the very least, firm and independent evidence would be needed to justify such a contention.

23 See Lance Roberts, "Understanding Affirmative Action," Discrimination, Affirmative Action, and Equal Opportunity, op. cit., pp. 147-182.

24 How else can we account for recommendation #10? This reads as follows:

>Employers should, with an assurance to their employees of confidentiality, be required to request and collect information on the participation in their workforces of women, native people (Status Indian, non-Status Indian, Metis, and Inuit), disabled persons, and specified ethnic and racial groups by occupational category, by salary quartile, and by salary range. This data should be filed annually with the enforcement agency.
>Data should also be collected on the representation of these groups in hirings, promotions, terminations, lay-offs, part-time work, contract work, internal task forces or committees, and training and educational leave opportunities. (p. 256)

25 This distinction can be illustrated by again analyzing the analogy mentioned above (see text accompanying Infra Note 18). Consider, once again, the "Jim Crow" laws

prevalent in the southern U.S. states of Alabama, Mississippi, and Georgia, etc., in the 1920s - 1940s. Based on this legislation, black people could not use certain water fountains, washrooms, and other such facilities. But then, under the spate of civil rights legislation of the 1960s, these enactments were swept into the dustbin of history, a fate they richly deserved. Ever since then, all such conveniences were by law open to all, regardless of race.

Suppose, however, as we did above, that we were to station "human rights" inspectors at each and every washroom and water fountain in the old confederate states, and found that only 5 percent of the users of these facilities were blacks (given that their representation in the total population was 12 percent). This, according to the logic of the AR, would not be "conclusive evidence of inequity." It would, rather, be "an effective signal that further examination is warranted to determine whether the disproportionately negative impact is in fact the result of inequitable practices, and therefore calls for remedial attention, or whether it is a reflection of a non-discriminatory reality," which presumably calls for no government action at all. What, in this case, might be considered an "inequitable practice"? One example would certainly be if the police forces refused to uphold the newer civil rights legislation, making a dead-letter law of them; instead, in this scenario, they might enforce the older Jim Crow law, and physically bar blacks from using the washrooms. This would be an obvious case of an "inequitable practice," calling for "remedial attention." Alternatively, the forces of law and order could turn a blind eye to gangs of racist hoodlums who harassed blacks using the facilities.

In stark contrast, what would be an instance of a "non-discriminatory reality" which might account for a black usage of water fountains, etc, of only 5 percent, given that they comprise 12 percent of the population? One possibility might be that comfort stations are located at airports, and that blacks utilize air travel to a lesser degree, proportionately, than do whites. In turn, there could be several explanations for such an occurrence: lower incomes, differing tastes, jobs which require fewer long distance trips, etc. Alternatively, it is conceivable that white air travellers might be older than black passengers, and might suffer from greater physical disability (kidney problems, nervous stomach, incontinence, bladder difficulties). If so, this would certainly be part of a "non-discriminatory reality," necessitating no public sector response whatsoever.

The point is, it would be of vital importance, given differential use of public facilities, to ascertain whether this was due to vestigial discriminatory practices (extortion, threats, violence) or to a "non-discriminatory reality." No stone should be left untouched to distinguish between these altogether different explanations for the behaviour observed. And this is precisely what the AR fails to do.

26 Thomas Sowell, "The Presuppositions of Affirmative Action," in Discrimination, Affirmative Action, and Equal Opportunity, op. cit., pp. 50, 51. We realize that public opinion is such that the mere mention of biological factors as an explanation for certain economic phenomena threatens to label the analyst in question as a racist or sexist. We thus salute Thomas Sowell for his courage as well as his perspicacity.

27 Ibid., p. 51.

28 See AR, p. 61.

29 Philip Blumstein and Pepper Schwartz, American Couples, New York: William Morrow & Co., 1983.

30 Newsweek, Sept. 19, 1983, p. 75.

31 The differential effects on high school boys and girls has been recognized by the Ontario educational authorities, who are taking special steps to stop the pattern of females dropping out of mathematics classes by grade 13. See Lorna Wiggen, Mathematics - The Invisible Filter: A Report on Math Avoidance, Math Anxiety, and Career Choices, Toronto Board of Education, 1983; Expanding Your Horizons in Mathematics and Science,

Berkley, California: Women's Center, Lawrence Hall of Science, 1979; Who Turns the Wheel, ed. Janet Ferguson, Ottawa: Science Council of Canada, 1982; Science for Every Student: Educating Canadians for Tomorrow's World, Ottawa: Science Council of Canada, Supply and Services Canada, 1984; see also Globe and Mail, October 26, 1984, pp. 1, 2.

32 See Table III.

33 Jesse Bernard, Academic Women, University Park, Pa.: Pennsylvania State University Press, 1964, p. 216.

34 Vivian Gornick, "Why Women Work," in Essays in Feminism, New York: Harper and Row, 1978, p. 87.

35 Dorothy Jongeward and Dru Scott, Women as Winners, London: Addison-Wesley, 1976, p. 15. Cited in Walter Block, "Economic Intervention, Discriminatrion, and Unforeseen Consequences," Discrimination, Affirmative Action, and Equal Opportunity, op. cit., pp. 246, 7.

36 These ratios, ranging from 34.2 percent to 49.7 percent, are far below those recorded by the AR. The difference is attributable to the fact that the AR reports income from employment only, on a full-time, full-year basis, while our data include all persons with income, from all sources. Ideally, it would have been preferable to use the same data, for purposes of comparison. But Statistics Canada does not offer a breakdown by marital status for full-time, full-year employment income. As well, it would have been preferable to have been able to cite data for the years between the census reports. This material is unpublished, unfortunately. It is available from Statistics Canada but only at a cost of $2980 for the years 1971-1983; for an additional $3000, the Fraser Institute would have been furnished with data for 1951, 1954, 1957, 1959, 1965 and 1967 (letter to Fraser Institute from Statistics Canada, dated April 9, 1985). Unfortunately, this was judged to be too expensive for our limited budget. The AR, with its budget in excess of $1,000,000 for this one study, might have made this information available to the public. But it chose not to,

perhaps unaware of the importance of marital status as an explanation of the male-female wage "gap."

37 Marriage enhances male and reduces female incomes, because of unequal child and house care responsibilities, and because the marriage partners act as a team, in effect raising total incomes, which are misleadingly assigned to the husband alone by our statisticians.

38 For example, our sample size in 1981 was as follows. Total: 15,809,930; ever-married: 11,791,675; never-married: 4,018,255. The ever-married thus comprised 74.6 percent of the population, while the figure for the never-married was 25.4 percent. Source: Census of 1981.

39 Walter Block, "Economic Intervention," op. cit., p. 112, found a female-male earnings ratio of .992 for a never-married sample which only very roughly adjusted for these four characteristics.

40 See text above, which accompanies Note 27.

41 Is this "progress," or not? In the traditional view of the wage gap, progress has been made in correcting the "imbalance," but much more remains to be done. The implicit premise here is that the struggle for equity will not be complete until the female-male ratio for all persons in Canada reaches the 100 percent level. That is to say, the present ratio of 49.7 percent must rise by 50.3 percentage points to 100 percent. But if this ever occurred, and the present mathematical relationship held firm, (that is, the increase in percentage terms was the same for the ever-married, the never-married, and all persons), then the female-male earnings ratio for never-married Canadians would have to rise to 94.2 percent, and that for the never-marrieds would have to skyrocket all the way up to 133.4 percent. A mighty strange "equity" indeed.

42 The allegation that employer discrimination is the main causal agent of the wage gap requires one to believe that male prejudice against hiring women fell in the 1940s,

rose in the 1950s, and fell again in the 1960s and 1970s. That, at least, is what must be maintained based on a perusal of the experience of the ever-married or of all persons. For this hypothesis, if confined to the "gap" for the never-marrieds, yields the result that employer discrimination decreased in the 1940s and 1950s, but then, inexplicably, increased in the 1960s and 1970s.

This "explanation" is reminiscent of the view that greed causes inflation; that greed increases when prices go up and decreases when they fall. See in this regard Jack Carr, "Wage and Price Controls: Panacea for Inflation or Prescription for Disaster?," The Illusion of Wage and Price Control, ed., Michael Walker, Vancouver: The Fraser Institute, 1976, p. 12.

43 It might be tempting to attribute the rise in the female-male income ratio for both never and ever-marrieds in 1941-1951 to the increased demand for female labour during World War II. But any such explanation is at best ambiguous, since this trend continued past the cessation of hostilities in 1946.

44 The Globe and Mail, March 22, 1985, pp. 1,2.

45 Women in Canada: A Statistical Report, Ottawa: Statistics Canada, 1985, Catalogue No. 89-503E.

46. The present authors have been engaged in an informal competition with Thomas Sowell (Civil Rights: Rhetoric or Reality, New York: William Morrow & Co., 1984; Affirmative Action Reconsidered, Washington, D.C.: American Enterprise Institute, 1975) as to which research could unearth the highest female-male income ratio. With 109.8 percent as our latest entry into the sweepstakes, we feel confident of eventual victory.

47 See in this regard Walter Williams "On Discrimination, Prejudice, Racial Income Differentials and Affirmative Action" in Discrimination, Affirmative Action, and Equal Opportunity, op. cit., pp. 69-99.

48 And this occurs, despite the additional tax revenues at their disposal. After all, bureaucrats are only human, with all the problems flesh is heir to.

49 Robert S. Smith, "Compensating Differentials and Public Policy," Industrial and Labour Relations Review, Vol. 32, April 1979, pp. 339-51; also see Gregory J. Duncan and Frank J. Stafford, "Do Union Members Receive Compensating Wage Differentials?," American Economic Review, Vol. 70, No. 3, June 1980, pp. 355-71.

50 And the same applies to women. Other things equal, they will accept lower pay for a job which puts them in contact with large numbers of eligible bachelors. There is no hard and fast sociological evidence showing that this phenomenon actually takes place. However, numerous "how to" manuals advocate such behaviour for their readers. See in this regard Helen Gurley Brown, Sex and the Single Girl, New York: Pocket Books, 1964, pp. 28-32; _____, Outrageous Opinions, New York: Avon, 1966, p. 54; "J," The Sensuous Woman, New York: Dell, 1971, chapter 17 "Where to Meet Men," especially p. 170.

51 As we shall see below, this is due in part to the recent move toward "equal pay for equal work" (EPFEW), and "equal pay for work of equal value" (EPFWOEV) legislation.

52 Richard B. Freeman, "Black Economic Progress After 1964: Who Has Gained?," cited in Walter Williams, "On Discrimination and Affirmative Action": in Discrimination, Affirmative Action, and Equal Opportunity, op. cit., p. 77.

53 Ibid., p. 77.

54 For an analysis which shows markets in a continual process of groping toward equilibrium -- but never quite reaching it, see Israel Kirzner, Competition and Entrepreneurship, Chicago: University of Chicago Press, 1973.

55 Several of the papers had multiple authors. This accounts for the numerical discrepancy.

56 See Table 2, p. 140, AR. The figure for 1981 was 28.1 percent, and for 1972-73, only 11.2 percent. There is no reliable data available describing the breakdown by gender for the economics profession as a whole.

57 This is likely to be an overestimate, since most of the prestigious authors involved in the AR probably have attained the Ph.D. degree in economics (this information is not given) and probably fewer than 28.4 percent of the practicing economics Ph.D.s in Canada are women.

58 These and many other similar points are made in a magnificant document entitled Minimum Wages: the New Issues in Theory, Evidence, Policy and Politics, Edwin G. West and Michael McKee, Ottawa: The Economic Council of Canada and the Institute for Research on Public Policy, 1980. Surveying the professional literature on the subject, these two Carleton University professors conclude that minimum wage laws in Canada have reduced employment opportunities of those at the bottom of the income scale. And they dismiss the policy of direct government job creations as a "second best" attempt to "mop up the damaging effects" created by this law in the first place. See also Walter Block, Focus: On Economics and the Canadian Bishops, Vancouver: The Fraser Institute, 1983, pp. 44 - 54; and Walter E. Williams, The State Against Blacks, New York: McGraw-Hill, 1982, for a superb analysis of minimum wage legislation and numerous other interferences with the rights of lesser skilled and downtrodden groups to attain employment status.

59 There is a second explanation for why such laws persist on the books, despite their obvious and deleterious effects upon the job prospects of the unskilled. This is the dismay with the fact that at today's prices, wages less than the minimum wage level would be insufficient to maintain anything like a dignified standard of living.

However, to look at the problem in this manner is to hopelessly mix apples and oranges. In determining the effects of minimum wage legislation on the well being of the unskilled, we must hold all other things constant, or, in the jargon of economists, insist upon ceteris paribus conditions. Let us consider the effects of the minimum wage law under two contrasing situations: the presence or the absence of welfare.

First, let us assume that there is no welfare payment at all. With a minimum wage law, the unskilled person is in dire straights indeed. He receives nothing from welfare, and nothing from employment, for a grand total of nothing (lower left hand box). Without welfare, and without wage legislation, the person's lot improves: he receives no welfare, but $80 from employment, for a sum of $80 (lower right hand box). We conclude, then, that in the absence of welfare, the non-minimum wage situation is vastly preferable to the minimum wage situation. $80 is preferable to 0.

Income received if welfare is:	Income received from work if minimum wage law is:	
	present	absent
present	150 + 0 = 150	150 + 80 = 230
absent	0 + 0 = 0	0 + 80 = 80

What about the condition of the poor if there are welfare payments of $150 per week? With wage legislation, the unskilled will receive $150 from welfare, and nothing from employment, for a total of $150 (upper left hand box). In contrast, without a minimum wage law, the person will receive $150 from welfare, and $80 from work, for a total of $230. Again, a minimum wage enactment is seen to be harmful: $230 is surely more desirable than $150.

A simplistic objection to the present analysis might argue as follows: since $150 is higher than $80, the minimum wage law helps the downtrodden. But as we have seen, it does no such thing. No matter how you slice it, with or without welfare, legislated minimum wages reduce the income of the poor. With welfare, $230 is better than $150; without, $80 is preferable to 0.

There is, however, a more sophisticated objection: under present law, it is impermissible in many jurisdictions to receive $150 from welfare plus $80 from work. If so, the entire upper right hand box is illegitimate.

This may well be true. But it is completely irrelevant to the point at issue. To reiterate: in order to determine the effects of minimum wage laws, it is imperative to hold all else constant. If welfare payments are allowed to vary (from 0 to $150, in our case), it is impossible to make a clear determination as to the effect of wage legislation. Only by comparing the presence or absence of minimum wages (with, and then without) welfare payments, as we have done, is there any hope of shedding light on this problem.

This concentration on money, of course, underestimates the true cost of minimum wages. For with work in the marketplace usually comes self-respect, independence, personal growth, on-the-job training, more skills, etc. With idleness and welfare there is the ever present threat of personal disintegration, dependency, alcoholism, crime, drug addiction. It is thus not inconceivable, even in this numerical example, to actually prefer the $80 receivable from work, to the $150 from welfare. Apart from these psychic aspects, the person who remains on welfare will always receive only the $150 (or rather whatever recompense is doled out); the employed person, in contrast, may possibly earn far more, eventually, as his investment in human capital rises.

60   Does this mean that those responsible for the AR are unfamiliar with their own bibliography? Additional serious challenges to this AR contention are cited in Note 9, Supra.

61   Morley Gunderson, The Female-Male Earnings Gap in Ontario: A Summary, Employment Information Series, No. 22 Toronto, Ontario Ministry of Labour, February 1982, p. 17.

62   Usually, within the same firm.

63 Morley Gunderson, "Male-Female Wage Differences in Ontario," A Report Prepared for the Ontario Ministry of Labour, December 1973, p. 103.

64 See Leon Louw, "Free Enterprise and the South African Black," Address to Barclay's Executive Womens Club, Johannesburg, South Africa, July 31, 1980, p. 4.

65 For a Canadian and non-racist analogue, see Ronald Hamowy, Canadian Medicine: A Study in Restricted Entry, Vancouver: The Fraser Institute, 1984.

66 One would think that when selecting the members for an eight person racing shell, only an objective criterion would be employed: picking the eight rowers who could displace the most water in a given time, as determined by mechanical calculation. Not so, not so. To be sure, this is one of the characteristics required, but so is an ability to work in smooth cohesion with the other seven rowers. As well, athletes are selected based on the following subjective assessments: ability to transcend ordinary output during a race, ability to give moral support to the other team members, etc.

67 All attempts to discern objective values -- whether for employment, goods, services, whatever -- have failed, and have failed miserably. For critiques of the medieval theory of "just price," and the Marxian attempt to establish "socially useful labour" as the objective measure of the value of goods and services, see Eugen von Bohm-Bawerk, "Value and Price," Book III, Volume II Capital and Interest, South Holland, Illinois: Libertarian Press, 1959.

68 We assume a necessarily segmented labour force; males cannot be hired to guard female prisoners, and females cannot be hired to guard male prisoners.

69 Walter Block, "Equal Pay Legislation," Ottawa, Economic Council, 1985.

70 Michael Levin, "Comparable Worth: The Feminist Road to Socialism," Commentary, Vol. 78, No. 3, September 1984, p. 16.

-110-

71 Recommendations 74-90, pp. 265-7, are devoted to job training.

72 For an institutional analysis of the marketplace and the government sector, comparing their respective abilities to pick industrial and employment "winners," see Kristian S. Palda, The Science Council's Weakest Link: A Critique of the Science Council's Technocratic Industrial Strategy for Canada, Vancouver: The Fraser Institute, 1979; _____, Industrial Innovation: Its Place in the Public Sector Policy Agenda, Vancouver: The Fraser Institute, 1984.

73 Vancouver Sun, January 8, 1982, page C7.

74 The figures in the text are based on extrapolations based on the model employed in "Legislation and the Labour Market: Canada," Ronald G. Bodkin and Andre Cournoyer, Unemployment Insurance: Global Evidence of Its Effects on Unemployment, Herbert G. Grubel and Michael A. Walker, eds., Vancouver: The Fraser Institute, 1978, pp. 82, 83. Actually, these figures are estimates of the unemployment encouraged by the 1971 expansion alone, and are thus an underestimate of the true rate of unemployment insurance induced unemployment in Canada.

75 For a comprehensive categorization of mobility barriers -- including union-imposed seniority rules and professional and trade licensing restrictions, social and education impediments -- see Canadian Confederation at the Crossroads, Michael A. Walker, ed., Vancouver: The Fraser Institute, 1978; also, Focus: On Alberta's Industrial and Science Strategy Proposals, Michael A. Walker, ed., Vancouver: The Fraser Institute, 1984.

76 See in this regard Dennis Maki, "An Evaluation of Canadian Federal Manpower Policies: Training and Job Creation, 1970-78," A Study Prepared for the Economic Council of Canada, 1978.

77 In a paragraph which can only be considered for the "understatement of the year award," the AR concedes as much. It reads as follows:

Labour market analysts, however, admit that even the most sophisticated projection systems are not totally adequate forecasters in emerging areas like microelectronics. Furthermore, there is no consensus on what sectors of the economy are likely to experience the largest growth over the next decade. (p. 159)

78 Conrad Winn, "Affirmative Action for Women: More than a Case of Simple Justice," Canadian Public Administration, Vol. 28, No. 1, Spring 1985, p. 24. Not only does Winn call for "equaliz(ing) income between genders," he also sees no problem in urging legislatively mandated EPFEW, and even EPFWOEV (see p. 35). Winn also favours government pay for housewives, and mandated changes in the tax code, the pension system, public education, and the job structure as an alternative means (to affirmative action) of equalizing income between the genders. Unfortunately, our concern in this monograph is only with the AR; space limitations, therefore, do not permit a critique of these proposals.

79 Ibid., pp. 30, 31, 32, 34, 35, 38, 39.

80 Ibid., p. 32.

81 Ibid., p. 34.

82 Ibid., p. 34, 35.

83 Ibid., p. 38.

84 Ibid., p. 39.

85 Ibid., p. 39.

86 New York Times, June 18, 1985, p. A12.

87 Ibid.

88 Globe & Mail, July 4, 1985, p. 1.